Decoding the TOEFL® iBT

Intermediate

SPEAKING

INTRODUCTION

For many learners of English, the TOEFL® iBT will be the most important standardized test they ever take. Unfortunately for a large number of these individuals, the material covered on the TOEFL® iBT remains a mystery to them, so they are unable to do well on the test. We hope that by using the *Decoding the TOEFL® iBT* series, individuals who take the TOEFL® iBT will be able to excel on the test and, in the process of using the book, may unravel the mysteries of the test and therefore make the material covered on the TOEFL® iBT more familiar to themselves.

The TOEFL® iBT covers the four main skills that a person must learn when studying any foreign language: reading, listening, speaking, and writing. The *Decoding the TOEFL® iBT* series contains books that cover all four of these skills. The *Decoding the TOEFL® iBT* series contains books with three separate levels for all four of the topics as well as the *Decoding the TOEFL® iBT Actual Test* books. These books are all designed to enable learners to utilize them to become better prepared to take the TOEFL® iBT. This book, *Decoding the TOEFL® iBT Speaking Intermediate*, covers the speaking aspect of the test. It is designed to help learners prepare for the Speaking section of the TOEFL® iBT.

Decoding the TOEFL® iBT Speaking Intermediate can be used by learners who are taking classes and also by individuals who are studying by themselves. It contains three parts and forty units. Part A covers the Independent Speaking Task (Question 1) while Part B and Part C cover the Integrated Speaking Tasks (Questions 2-4). There is also one actual test at the end of the book. Each unit has either two independent questions or two integrated questions. It also contains exercises designed to help learners understand how to present the best possible responses for the Speaking section. The passages and questions in *Decoding the TOEFL® iBT Speaking Intermediate* are slightly lower levels than those found on the TOEFL® iBT. Individuals who use *Decoding the TOEFL® iBT Speaking Intermediate* will therefore be able to prepare themselves not only to take the TOEFL® iBT but also to perform well on the test.

We hope that everyone who uses *Decoding the TOEFL® iBT Speaking Intermediate* will be able to become more familiar with the TOEFL® iBT and will additionally improve his or her score on the test. As the title of the book implies, we hope that learners can use it to crack the code on the TOEFL® iBT, to make the test itself less mysterious and confusing, and to get the highest grade possible. Finally, we hope that both learners and instructors can use this book to its full potential. We wish all of you the best of luck as you study English and prepare for the TOEFL® iBT, and we hope that *Decoding the TOEFL® iBT Speaking Intermediate* can provide you with assistance during the course of your studies.

Michael A. Putlack
Stephen Poirier
Tony Covello

TABLE
OF
CONTENTS

Part A **Independent Speaking Task** 11

Question 1 14

Part B **Integrated Speaking Tasks**
Reading, Listening, and Speaking 45

Question 2 51
Question 3 81

Part C **Integrated Speaking Task**
Listening and Speaking 111

Question 4 115

Actual Test 145

ABOUT THE TOEFL® iBT SPEAKING SECTION

How the Section Is Organized

The Speaking section is the third part of the TOEFL® iBT and consists of four questions. Question 1 is called the Independent Speaking Task and asks test takers to speak about a familiar topic. The other questions, questions 2-4, are called the Integrated Speaking Tasks. These tasks require test takers to integrate their speaking skills with other language skills such as listening and reading skills.

For each of the four questions, test takers are given preparation time and response time. During the preparation time, test takers can write down brief notes about how they will organize their responses. The preparation time ranges from 15 to 30 seconds, and the response time is either 45 or 60 seconds. The spoken responses are recorded and sent to be scored by raters. The raters evaluate responses based on three criteria: Delivery (how clear your speech is), Language Use (how effectively you use grammar and vocabulary to convey your ideas), and Topic Development (how fully you answer the question and how coherently you present your ideas).

Changes in the Speaking Section

The Speaking section is the section that has gone through the most drastic changes. Two question types—Questions 1 and 5 on the old test—have been removed. Therefore, the total number of questions has become four instead of six. Accordingly, the time allotted for the Speaking section has been reduced from 20 minutes to 17 minutes. However, the remaining questions have no changes, and the preparation times and the response times remain the same.

Question Types

TYPE 1 Independent Speaking Task: Question 1

The first question asks test takers to speak about a familiar topic. It is necessary for test takers to include specific examples and details in their response. After the question is presented, test takers are given 15 seconds to prepare their response and 45 seconds to speak.

Question 1 asks test takers to make a personal choice between two possible opinions, actions, or situations. In addition, on recent tests, test takers are sometimes given three options from which to choose, and they may be asked to speak about both the advantages and the disadvantages of a particular topic. Test takers are required to explain their choice by providing reasons and details. Topics for this question include everyday issues of general interest to test takers. For example, the question may ask about a preference between studying at home and studying at the library, a preference between living in a dormitory and living in an off-campus apartment, or a preference between a class with a lot of discussion and one without discussion.

ABOUT THE TOEFL® iBT SPEAKING SECTION

TYPE 2 Integrated Speaking Tasks (Reading, Listening, and Speaking): **Questions 2 and 3**

The second and third questions require test takers to integrate different language skills. Test takers are first presented with a short reading passage. The time given for reading is 45-50 seconds. After that, test takers will listen to a conversation or a lecture which is related to information presented in the reading passage. They need to organize their response by using information from both the reading passage and the conversation or lecture. For these questions, test takers are given 30 seconds to prepare their response and 60 seconds to speak.

Question 2 concerns a topic of campus-related interest, but it does not require prior firsthand experience of college or university life in North America to understand the topic. The reading passage is usually between 75 and 100 words long. It may be an announcement, letter, or article regarding a policy, rule, or future plan of a college or university. It can also be related to campus facilities or the quality of life on campus. After reading the passage, test takers will listen to two speakers discuss the topic presented in the reading passage. Typically, one of the two speakers shows a strong opinion about the topic. On recent tests, however, speakers have shown mixed feelings about the topic, so they like it yet also dislike some aspect of it. Test takers need to summarize the speaker's opinion and the reasons for holding it.

In Question 3, test takers will read a short passage about an academic subject and then listen to a professor lecture about that subject. The question requires test takers to relate the reading passage and the lecture. Topics for this question can be drawn from a variety of fields, including life science, social science, physical science, and the humanities. However, the question does not require prior knowledge of any particular field.

TYPE 3 Integrated Speaking Tasks (Listening and Speaking): **Question 4**

The last question presents only a listening passage—a lecture—and not a reading passage. Test takers need to respond based on what they hear. They are given 20 seconds to prepare their response and 60 seconds to speak.

For Question 4, test takers will listen to a lecture about an academic topic. As in Question 3, topics for this question can be drawn from a variety of fields, including life science, social science, physical science, and the humanities. Again, no prior knowledge is necessary to understand the lecture. After hearing the lecture, test takers are asked to summarize the lecture and to explain how the examples are connected with the overall topic.

HOW TO USE THIS BOOK

Decoding the TOEFL® iBT Speaking Intermediate is designed to be used either as a textbook in a classroom environment or as a study guide for individual learners. There are 3 parts and 40 units in this book. Each unit provides 2 sample questions, which enable you to build up your skills on a particular speaking task. At the end of the book, there is one actual test of the Speaking section of the TOEFL® iBT.

 Part A **Independent Speaking Task**

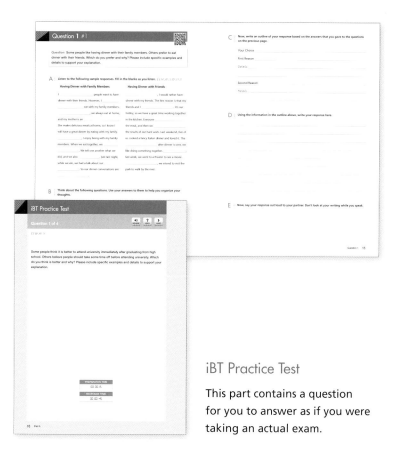

This section has a Speaking question followed by sample responses with blanks for you to fill in as you listen to them. This is followed by brainstorming questions and spaces to write an outline and a sample answer.

iBT Practice Test

This part contains a question for you to answer as if you were taking an actual exam.

Part B — Integrated Speaking Tasks: Reading, Listening, and Speaking

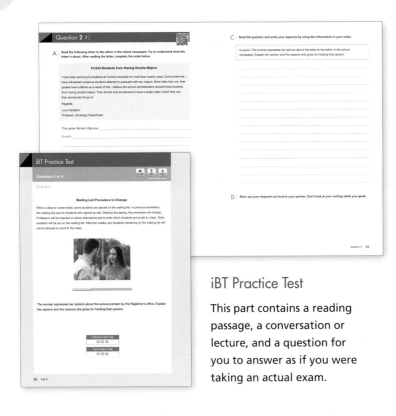

This part has a reading passage followed by either a conversation or lecture. There are spaces to take notes on the passage and the conversation or lecture. This is followed by a space to write your own sample answer.

iBT Practice Test

This part contains a reading passage, a conversation or lecture, and a question for you to answer as if you were taking an actual exam.

Part C — Integrated Speaking Task: Listening and Speaking

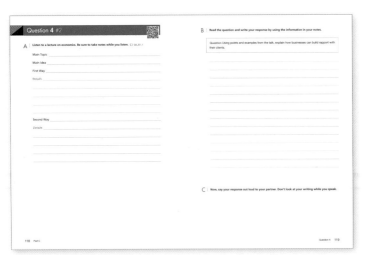

This part has a lecture. There is space to take notes on the lecture. This is followed by a space to write your own sample answer.

iBT Practice Test

This part contains a lecture and a question for you to answer as if you were taking an actual exam.

● **Actual Test** (at the end of the book)

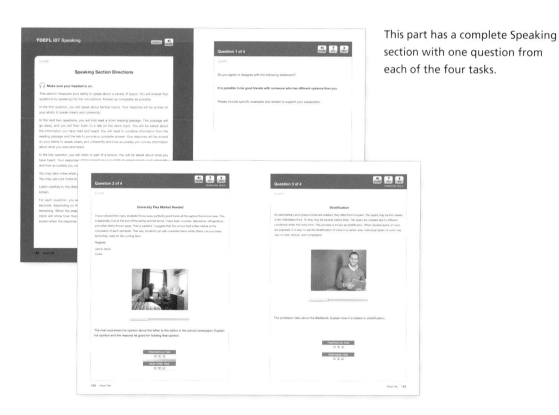

This part has a complete Speaking section with one question from each of the four tasks.

Part A

Independent Speaking Task
Question 1

Independent Speaking Task

◢ About the Task

The Independent Speaking Task asks test takers to speak about familiar topics. It is necessary for test takers to include specific examples and details in their response. After the question is presented, test takers are given 15 seconds to prepare their response and 45 seconds to speak.

The Independent Speaking Task is the first question (question 1) of the Speaking section.

Question 1 asks test takers to make a personal choice between two possible opinions, actions, or situations. Test takers are required to explain their choice by providing reasons and details. Topics for this question include everyday issues of general interest to test takers. For example, the question may ask about a preference between studying at home and studying at the library, a preference between living in a dormitory and living in an off-campus apartment, or a preference between a class with a lot of discussion and one without discussion.

When you answer the question, be sure to use examples. Personal examples involving family members are ideal. The examples you use do not have to be actual events that occurred, but you should present them that way. You merely need to provide examples that defend the argument you are making. In addition, do not discuss both sides for the question. Make your choice and speak only about it.

◪ Sample Question

VOLUME　HELP　NEXT

🎧 Q1_00_1

Do you agree or disagree with the following statement?

It is important for children to spend a short period of time living far from home while staying with relatives or friends.

Please include specific examples and details to support your explanation.

PREPARATION TIME
00:00:15

RESPONSE TIME
00:00:45

Sample Response   🎧 Q1_00_2

I agree with the statement. I think it's important for children to spend some time living away from home at a friend's or relative's house. First of all, this can help the child gain some independence. When I was young, I stayed at my grandparents' home one summer. It was a great experience because I learned how to be away from my parents for a while. Second of all, living in another place is fun. I had a wonderful experience at my grandparents' home. They live in the countryside, so I went fishing and swimming every day. I also did lots of other fun outdoor activities with them.

> **Question** Some people like having dinner with their family members. Others prefer to eat dinner with their friends. Which do you prefer and why? Please include specific examples and details to support your explanation.

A | Listen to the following sample responses. Fill in the blanks as you listen. 🎧 Q1_01_1, Q1_01_2

Having Dinner with Family Members

I _____ people want to have dinner with their friends. However, I _____ _____ eat with my family members. _____, we always eat at home, and my mother is an _____ . She makes delicious meals at home, so I know I will have a great dinner by eating with my family. _____, I enjoy being with my family members. When we eat together, we _____ _____ . We tell one another what we did, and we also _____ . Just last night, while we ate, we had a talk about our _____ _____ . So our dinner conversations are _____ .

Having Dinner with Friends

_____, I would rather have dinner with my friends. The first reason is that my friends and I _____ . It's our hobby, so we have a great time working together in the kitchen. Everyone _____ the meal, and then we _____ the results of our hard work. Last weekend, five of us cooked a fancy Italian dinner and loved it. The _____ after dinner is over, we like doing something together. _____, last week, we went to a theater to see a movie. _____, we intend to visit the park to walk by the river.

B | Think about the following questions. Use your answers to them to help you organize your thoughts.

Having Dinner with Family Members

❶ Why do you like having dinner with your family members?

❷ Where do you usually eat with them?

❸ What do you talk about at dinner?

Having Dinner with Friends

❶ Why do you like having dinner with your friends?

❷ Where do you have dinner with them?

❸ What do you do after dinner?

C Now, write an outline of your response based on the answers that you gave to the questions on the previous page.

Your Choice _____

First Reason _____

Details _____

_____

Second Reason _____

Details _____

_____

D Using the information in the outline above, write your response here.

_____

_____

_____

_____

_____

_____

_____

_____

E Now, say your response out loud to your partner. Don't look at your writing while you speak.

iBT Practice Test

🎧 Q1_01_3

Some people think it is better to attend university immediately after graduating from high school. Others believe people should take some time off before attending university. Which do you think is better and why? Please include specific examples and details to support your explanation.

PREPARATION TIME
00:00:15

RESPONSE TIME
00:00:45

> **Question** Do you agree or disagree with the following statement?
> **The government should regulate television programs with excessive violence or bad language.**
> Please include specific examples and details to support your explanation.

A | Listen to the following sample responses. Fill in the blanks as you listen. 🎧 Q1_02_1, Q1_02_2

Agree

Nowadays, there are countless programs on television with excessive violence and bad language. I believe the government _____ regulate those shows. First off, many children accidentally turn the channel to these shows and wind up watching them. Children _____ be exposed to that kind of adult content. Once when I was young, I watched a show with bad language _____ _____. My parents were so upset about that. _____, shows with excessive violence and language are bad _____ on people, especially teenagers. For example, teenagers _____ the things they see on television, so they develop poor morals. I don't want that to happen, so these shows need to be regulated.

Disagree

I _____ the government should regulate any television programs. _____ _____, people have the right to choose what they want to do. The government _____ _____ to tell people what they should or should not watch. If people want to watch movies with lots of violence and bad language, they should _____ do so. _____ _____, I understand that parents don't want their children exposed to these programs. But it's their _____ to monitor what their children are watching. My parents _____ _____ that my sister and I didn't watch any bad shows. They didn't _____ the government _____ them.

B | Think about the following questions. Use your answers to them to help you organize your thoughts.

Agree

1. Why do you think the government should regulate television programs?
2. Who can be harmed by these programs?
3. What kinds of bad effects can these programs have?

Disagree

1. Why do you think the government should not regulate television programs?
2. What is your opinion on government involvement in people's lives?
3. How can parents keep their children from watching certain television programs?

C Now, write an outline of your response based on the answers that you gave to the questions on the previous page.

Your Choice _____

First Reason _____

Details _____

_____

Second Reason _____

Details _____

_____

D Using the information in the outline above, write your response here.

_____

_____

_____

_____

_____

_____

_____

_____

_____

E Now, say your response out loud to your partner. Don't look at your writing while you speak.

iBT Practice Test

🎧 Q1_02_3

Do you agree or disagree with the following statement?

Bosses and workers should be close to one another.

Please include specific examples and details to support your explanation.

PREPARATION TIME
00:00:15

RESPONSE TIME
00:00:45

> **Question** Which did you prefer when you were young, staying at home on the weekend or visiting a relative's house? Please include specific examples and details to support your explanation.

A | Listen to the following sample responses. Fill in the blanks as you listen. 🎧 Q1_03_1, Q1_03_2

Staying at Home

When I was young, I always _____ stay at home on the weekend. First, I got the _____ to spend time with my parents. Both of my parents worked, so they couldn't do many _____ with me on weekdays. _____, on weekends, my parents and I always spent time together. That _____ _____ become close to my parents. _____ when I was young, I loved playing computer games. My parents bought me a computer, and they _____ play computer games for an hour or two on the weekend. That was also a _____ which I could only do at my home.

Visiting a Relative's House

There was _____ visiting a relative's house on the weekend when I was young. My grandparents lived an hour away from us, so we _____ to their home. They had _____ for my brothers and me. My grandmother also always cooked delicious food for us. I have very _____ _____ of visiting their house as a child. We used to go to my uncle's home. too. He has two sons, so my brothers, _____, and I would go to the park and play sports. We played basketball and soccer for several hours each day. Those were some of the _____ _____.

B | Think about the following questions. Use your answers to them to help you organize your thoughts.

Staying at Home

1. Why did you prefer to stay at home on the weekend?
2. Who did you spend time with?
3. What did you do with them?

Visiting a Relative's House

1. Why did you prefer to visit a relative's house on the weekend?
2. Which relative did you like to visit?
3. What did you do at that relative's house?

C Now, write an outline of your response based on the answers that you gave to the questions on the previous page.

Your Choice

First Reason

Details

Second Reason

Details

D Using the information in the outline above, write your response here.

E Now, say your response out loud to your partner. Don't look at your writing while you speak.

iBT Practice Test

🎧 Q1_03_3

Which would you prefer, to have your own business or to work for another person? Please include specific examples and details to support your explanation.

PREPARATION TIME
00:00:15

RESPONSE TIME
00:00:45

> **Question** Do you agree or disagree with the following statement?
>
> **Teachers should give students lots of assignments.**
>
> Please include specific examples and details to support your explanation.

A Listen to the following sample responses. Fill in the blanks as you listen. 🎧 Q1_04_1, Q1_04_2

Agree

I think teachers _____ give their students lots of assignments, so I _____ the statement. First of all, teachers have to _____ _____ their students understand the material being taught. The best way to do this is to give students homework. When teachers check homework, they can _____ if the students know the material or don't understand it. Then, they can _____ move on to new material or go over the old material again. Next, assignments are a great way for students to improve _____. I must often _____ to complete my school assignments. When doing that, I learn more and therefore become more _____.

Disagree

Most people _____ with this statement, but I _____ it. To begin with, students these days are _____ _____. I have between three and four hours of homework every day. If all of my teachers give many assignments, then I'll become _____ _____. I probably won't even have enough time to finish my homework every day. _____ is that a great deal of homework is merely busy work. _____, math teachers love assigning problems for students to solve. But if the students understand the material, there's _____ _____ to do twenty or thirty problems. Solving ten problems is _____.

B Think about the following questions. Use your answers to them to help you organize your thoughts.

Agree

1. Why do you think teachers should give their students lots of assignments?
2. What kinds of assignments should teachers give?
3. How can assignments benefit students?

Disagree

1. Why do you think teachers should not give their students lots of assignments?
2. How can too many assignments harm students?
3. How should teachers test their students' knowledge?

C
Now, write an outline of your response based on the answers that you gave to the questions on the previous page.

Your Choice

First Reason

Details

Second Reason

Details

D
Using the information in the outline above, write your response here.

E
Now, say your response out loud to your partner. Don't look at your writing while you speak.

🎧 Q1_04_3

Do you agree or disagree with the following statement?

Playing sports at young ages can make children become competitive as they get older.

Please include specific examples and details to support your explanation.

PREPARATION TIME
00:00:15

RESPONSE TIME
00:00:45

Question Do you agree or disagree with the following statement?

Students should be allowed to eat snacks in class.

Please include specific examples and details to support your explanation.

A | **Listen to the following sample responses. Fill in the blanks as you listen.** Q1_05_1, Q1_05_2

Agree

I _____ with the statement. Students like myself are busy _____, and we sometimes don't have time to eat breakfast or lunch. _____, it would be great if we were allowed to eat snacks during class. That would _____ getting too hungry. _____, snacks can provide students with energy when they need it. _____, I was starving in the middle of class. When my teacher wasn't looking, I ate a quick snack. I _____ do that. But I felt much better afterward. Since I was able to _____ in class, I didn't feel bad about eating in class.

Disagree

Students should never _____ eat snacks in class. I _____ disagree with the statement. _____ students skip breakfast or lunch, they have time to eat snacks. At my school, there are five minutes between each class. That's _____ to eat a small snack. So there's no need to have any snacks during class. Second, if students eat snacks in class, they will cause disruptions. _____ _____, the students eating the snacks won't pay attention to the lesson. _____ _____, they won't learn anything. _____, they'll disturb the class by eating, so other students won't be able to _____ the teacher.

B | **Think about the following questions. Use your answers to them to help you organize your thoughts.**

Agree

❶ Why should students be allowed to eat snacks in class?

❷ Why might students need to eat snacks in class?

❸ How can eating snacks in class help students?

Disagree

❶ Why should students not be allowed to eat snacks in class?

❷ When should students eat snacks?

❸ How can students eating snacks in class cause problems?

C   **Now, write an outline of your response based on the answers that you gave to the questions on the previous page.**

Your Choice _____

First Reason _____

Details _____

_____

Second Reason _____

Details _____

_____

D   **Using the information in the outline above, write your response here.**

_____

_____

_____

_____

_____

_____

_____

_____

_____

_____

E   **Now, say your response out loud to your partner. Don't look at your writing while you speak.**

iBT Practice Test

🎧 Q1_05_3

Which do you prefer, doing exercise every day or exercising only when you have free time? Please include specific examples and details to support your explanation.

PREPARATION TIME
00:00:15

RESPONSE TIME
00:00:45

Question Answer one of the following questions.

1 Some people prefer to be very good at one activity while others prefer to be above average at several activities. Talk about the advantages and disadvantages of being very good at one activity. Use details and examples to explain your answer.

2 Some people prefer to be very good at one activity while others prefer to be above average at several activities. Talk about the advantages and disadvantages of being above average at several activities. Use details and examples to explain your answer.

A | **Listen to the following sample responses. Fill in the blanks as you listen.** 🎧 Q1_06_1, Q1_06_2

Being Very Good at One Activity

There are _____ being very good at one activity. _____, you could probably make money from that activity. My cousin _____. He's an outstanding baseball player and might become a pro ballplayer one day. _____ become famous because they can do a single activity very well. There are some _____ though. _____ a person might get bored with that activity and not want to do it anymore. Then, that person _____ _____ another activity well. Some people also might only talk about _____ with their friends. Their friends might not enjoy hearing about the same topic again and again.

Being Above Average at Several Activities

I can think of _____ to being above average at several activities. Because a person can do several things well, that person can _____. My brother is a member of several clubs, and his friends are _____. A person who's above average at several activities can also _____ _____. So that person will always be able to get a job. _____, people who are only above average will never become _____. That could destroy the dreams of some people. They will also never become _____ since they focus on many different activities.

B | **Think about the following questions. Use your answers to them to help you organize your thoughts**

Being Very Good at One Activity

❶ How can being very good at one activity help a person?

Being Above Average at Several Activities

❶ How can being above average at several activities help a person?

② How can the lack of ability at other activities be harmful?

② How can being above average at several activities be harmful?

C | **Now, write an outline of your response based on the answers that you gave to the previous questions.**

Topic Sentence _____

First Reason _____

Details _____

_____

Second Reason _____

Details _____

_____

D | **Using the information in the outline above, write your response here.**

_____

_____

_____

_____

_____

_____

_____

_____

_____

E | **Now, say your response out loud to your partner. Don't look at your writing while you speak.**

Q1_06_3

Answer one of the following questions.

1   Some students prefer buying textbooks for their classes while others prefer checking the books they need out from the library. Talk about the advantages and disadvantages of buying textbooks for classes. Use details and examples to explain your answer.

2   Some students prefer buying textbooks for their classes while others prefer checking the books they need out from the library. Talk about the advantages and disadvantages of checking out books from the library for classes. Use details and examples to explain your answer.

PREPARATION TIME
00 : 00 : 15

RESPONSE TIME
00 : 00 : 45

> **Question** You are going to take a trip by yourself to a foreign country. Which of the following will you do?
>
> • Tell all of your friends and family members where you are going
> • Tell one or two friends or family members where you are going
> • Tell nobody where you are going
>
> Use details and examples to explain your answer.

A | Listen to the following sample responses. Fill in the blanks as you listen. 🎧 Q1_07_1, Q1_07_2

Tell All of My Friends and Family Members

_____ all my friends and family members where I'm going. _____ some of my friends and family members might have visited the country before. So _____ about good places to go. For instance, my uncle is a _____. He has visited dozens of countries and can recommend interesting _____ _____. I also don't want to just disappear for a while. It would be rude _____ people where I'm going. Once, one of my friends traveled abroad for six months but didn't tell anyone. _____ and thought something bad had happened. I don't want people to worry about me like that.

Tell One or Two Friends or Family Members

I would tell one or two friends or family members where I'm going. _____ , I'm a private person, so I don't need to tell everyone _____ _____. I can tell my parents and best friend what I'm doing. Then, they won't worry while I'm gone. _____ , I don't want people to think I'm _____ traveling abroad. One of my classmates travels abroad frequently. He's very _____ _____ and often discusses his trips. Some people think he's _____ because he can afford to travel so much. I don't want people to _____ , so I wouldn't discuss traveling unless people asked me about it.

B | Think about the following questions. Use your answers to them to help you organize your thoughts.

Tell All of My Friends and Family Members

❶ Why is is important to tell everyone about your trip?
❷ How would that benefit you?

Tell One or Two Friends or Family Members

❶ Why would you only tell a few people about your trip?
❷ What are the advantages of doing that?

Tell Nobody

❶ Why would you tell nobody about your trip?

❷ What are the advantages of keeping details of a trip secret?

C **Now, write an outline of your response based on the answers that you gave to the previous questions.**

Topic Sentence _____

First Reason _____

Details _____

_____

Second Reason _____

Details _____

_____

D **Using the information in the outline above, write your response here.**

_____

_____

_____

_____

_____

_____

_____

_____

E **Now, say your response out loud to your partner. Don't look at your writing while you speak.**

iBT Practice Test

🎧 Q1_07_3

Your city has received a large donation of money. How should it spend that money?

- By repairing roads
- By building a new park
- By expanding the local museum

Use details and examples to explain your answer.

PREPARATION TIME
00:00:15

RESPONSE TIME
00:00:45

> **Question** Do you agree or disagree with the following statement?
> **People with a lot of free time should spend some of it doing volunteer work.**
> Use details and examples to explain your answer.

A   Listen to the following sample responses. Fill in the blanks as you listen. 🎧 Q1_08_1, Q1_08_2

Agree

I _____ the statement. People with a free time should spend some of it doing volunteer work. First, there's a _____ _____ everywhere. Many people want to volunteer but are _____ _____ work and family. So people with free time should help _____. My aunt is a housewife _____ are in college. She has lots of free time, so she volunteers at a _____. In addition, people with plenty of free time _____ _____. So they can make themselves busy _____. They might even learn a _____ if they volunteer at a hospital or similar place.

Disagree

I _____ people with free time need to volunteer, so I _____ the statement. First, volunteer work should be _____. People shouldn't volunteer because others _____ them or _____ them to do that. Some local schools _____ students to volunteer. That's not really volunteering, so I think it's _____ for the schools to _____ students do it. Second, everyone has _____ of spending free time. Some people may want to volunteer _____ may prefer to play sports or just stay at home and relax. Everyone is _____. So it's not right to expect people to volunteer _____ they have some free time.

B   Think about the following questions. Use your answers to them to help you organize your thoughts.

Agree

1. What volunteer work would you like to do?
2. Why do you think people should do volunteer work?

Disagree

1. Why is it wrong to make people do volunteer work?
2. What do you prefer to do in your free time?

C Now, write an outline of your response based on the answers that you gave to the questions on the previous page.

Topic Sentence _____

First Reason _____

Details _____

_____

Second Reason _____

Details _____

_____

D Using the information in the outline above, write your response here.

_____

_____

_____

_____

_____

_____

_____

_____

_____

E Now, say your response out loud to your partner. Don't look at your writing while you speak.

iBT Practice Test

Q1_08_3

Answer one of the following questions.

1   Some people prefer shopping for groceries at supermarkets while others prefer visiting specialty stores such as butcher shops and bakeries. Talk about the advantages and disadvantages of shopping at supermarkets. Use details and examples to explain your answer.

2   Some people prefer shopping for groceries at supermarkets while others prefer visiting specialty stores such as butcher shops and bakeries. Talk about the advantages and disadvantages of shopping at specialty stores such as butcher shops and bakeries. Use details and examples to explain your answer.

PREPARATION TIME
00:00:15

RESPONSE TIME
00:00:45

> **Question** Which of the following should supervisors at companies do?
>
> • Help their employees with their professional development
> • Let their employees work the way they want to
>
> Use details and examples to explain your answer.

A | Listen to the following sample responses. Fill in the blanks as you listen. 🎧 Q1_09_1, Q1_09_2

Help Their Employees with Their Personal Development

For me, the choice is _____ . Supervisors should help their employees with their professional development. The _____ is that they can teach their employees _____ _____ their jobs better. Supervisors have lots of _____ and know how to work well. They should _____ their workers _____ some of their knowledge. _____ _____ is that this will help the overall _____ of a company. My mother is a supervisor at her company. She always _____ her employees _____ their jobs. As a result, her department's _____ has increased very much. This has _____ her company to do well and to make lots of money.

Let Their Employees Work the Way They Want To

I believe supervisors _____ their employees work the way they want to. First, supervisors don't know _____ _____ every job at a company. So they might give bad _____ or _____ to some workers. My brother's _____ does this. He often tells my brother to do something, but it's bad advice. My brother has to _____ the instructions though because he can't _____ his boss. In addition, there are usually _____ to do tasks. And everyone is different. It's _____ _____ let workers be creative and do work according to the style that _____ . Good supervisors realize this and _____ their employees _____ .

B | Think about the following questions. Use your answers to them to help you organize your thoughts.

Help Their Employees with Their Personal Development

❶ How can employees improve their professional development?

Let Their Employees Work the Way They Want To

❶ Why do some employees like to work their own way?

❷ How can supervisors help their employees?   ❷ What are some benefits of employees working their own way?

C · Now, write an outline of your response based on the answers that you gave to the previous questions.

Topic Sentence _____

First Reason _____

Details _____

_____

Second Reason _____

Details _____

_____

D · Using the information in the outline above, write your response here.

_____

_____

_____

_____

_____

_____

_____

_____

_____

_____

_____

E · Now, say your response out loud to your partner. Don't look at your writing while you speak.

iBT Practice Test

VOLUME   HELP   NEXT

Q1_09_3

You need spending money for when you go to university. Which of the following will you do to get money?

- Work part time during the semester
- Work full time during summer vacation
- Take out a loan from a bank

Use details and examples to explain your answer.

PREPARATION TIME
00:00:15

RESPONSE TIME
00:00:45

Question Answer one of the following questions.

1 Some people prefer always to tell the truth while others prefer to be more polite at times. Talk about the advantages and disadvantages of always telling the truth. Use details and examples to explain your answer.

2 Some people prefer always to tell the truth while others prefer to be more polite at times. Talk about the advantages and disadvantages of being more polite at times. Use details and examples to explain your answer.

A Listen to the following sample responses. Fill in the blanks as you listen. 🎧 Q1_10_1, Q1_10_2

Always Telling the Truth

I can think of some _____ always telling the truth. One is that people will believe _____ _____. My brother is honest even when it could _____ him. People know that, so they believe _____. In addition, people ask honest individuals for _____ all the time. They know they will hear the truth _____ _____ it might be unwelcome or unpleasant. There are disadvantages though. Sometimes people can _____ by the truth. My brother sometimes tells people their clothes _____ or their hair is unstylish. That can hurt their _____. In cases like those, telling _____ would be a bit more convenient.

Being More Polite at Times

One advantage of being more polite at times is that a person can _____ good. My friend asked me about some cookies she made once. They _____, but I said they were good. Because I was _____, she was happy. It's also sometimes better to be polite than to be _____. There were no advantages to telling my friend the truth about her cookies. _____, being polite can harm some people. One time, I told a different friend that he was _____ drawing pictures even though he wasn't. He _____ an art contest, and people _____ his pictures. He felt _____ bad _____ he never drew pictures again.

B Think about the following questions. Use your answers to them to help you organize your thoughts.

Always Telling the Truth

❶ Why do some people tell the truth?

Being More Polite at Times

❶ Why is it important to be polite to others?

❷ How can telling the truth hurt people at times?

❷ How can being polite to others cause problems?

C | **Now, write an outline of your response based on the answers that you gave to the previous questions.**

Topic Sentence _____

First Reason _____

Details _____

_____

Second Reason _____

Details _____

_____

D | **Using the information in the outline above, write your response here.**

_____

_____

_____

_____

_____

_____

_____

_____

_____

E | **Now, say your response out loud to your partner. Don't look at your writing while you speak.**

iBT Practice Test

🎧 Q1_10_3

Answer one of the following questions.

1   Some people prefer to use public transportation when they go on trips while others prefer to rent a car to get around. Talk about the advantages and disadvantages of using public transportation while on a trip. Use details and examples to explain your answer.

2   Some people prefer to use public transportation when they go on trips while others prefer to rent a car to get around. Talk about the advantages and disadvantages of renting a car while on a trip. Use details and examples to explain your answer.

PREPARATION TIME
00:00:15

RESPONSE TIME
00:00:45

Part **B**

Integrated Speaking Tasks
Reading, Listening, and Speaking

Questions 2 & 3

Integrated Speaking Tasks | Reading, Listening, and Speaking

◢ About the Tasks

The second and third questions require test takers to integrate different language skills. Test takers are first presented with a short reading passage. The time given for reading is 45 seconds. After that, test takers will listen to a conversation or a lecture which is related to information presented in the reading passage. They need to organize their response by using information from both the reading passage and the conversation or lecture. For these questions, test takers are given 30 seconds to prepare their response and 60 seconds to speak.

Question 2 concerns a topic of campus-related interest, but it does not require prior firsthand experience of college or university life in North America to understand the topic. The reading passage is usually between 75 and 100 words long. It may be an announcement, letter, or article regarding a policy, rule, or future plan of a college or university. It can also be related to campus facilities or the quality of life on campus. After reading the passage, test takers will listen to two speakers discuss the topic presented in the reading passage. Typically, one of the two speakers shows a strong opinion about the topic. Test takers need to summarize the speaker's opinion and the reasons for holding it.

In **Question 3**, test takers will read a short passage about an academic subject and then listen to a professor lecture about that subject. The question requires test takers to relate the reading passage and the lecture. Topics for this question can be drawn from a variety of fields, including life science, social science, physical science, and the humanities. However, the question does not require prior knowledge of any particular field.

When you answer the questions, be sure to use only the information that is presented in the reading passage and conversation or lecture. Even if you possess outside knowledge of the topic, you should not use it. In addition, when listening to the speakers, focus specifically on the one who is expressing a strong opinion about the topic. Ignore whatever the other person says. As for the professor, pay close attention to the examples he or she gives and then use them to show how the lecture is related to the reading passage.

🎧 Q2_00_1

Snacks to Be Sold on Movie Night

Every Wednesday night, Central University's only movie club, Movie Central, shows two feature films. Starting on Wednesday, January 18, snacks will be sold during the showing. Popcorn, chocolate, candy bars, and drinks will be sold in the lobby of Weston Hall. Snacks may be purchased any time thirty minutes before each movie starts and fifteen minutes after they begin. All proceeds will go to the school's Performing Arts Department.

The woman expresses her opinion about the announcement by the student activities office. Explain her opinion and the reasons she gives for holding that opinion.

PREPARATION TIME
00:00:30

RESPONSE TIME
00:00:60

Now listen to two students discussing the announcement.

M Student: Hey, great news. We can buy food and drinks on movie night now. I can't wait to see the first showing of the semester.

W Student: You're pleased about that?

M: Of course. After all, uh, what's a movie without popcorn?

W: Personally, I wish snacks weren't being sold. For one thing, the food and drinks will be a major distraction.

M: Huh? How so?

W: You know . . . People will have to smell the popcorn. That's annoying, especially for people who don't purchase any. And the noise of people eating and drinking will prevent people from enjoying the movie.

M: Er . . . I never really considered that.

W: Plus, the money is just going to be turned over to a school department. They shouldn't do that. I don't like that the school will make more money off us. Tuition is already high enough. The money should be donated to charity.

M: Yeah, I suppose you have a good point there.

Sample Response Q2_00_2

The speakers have a conversation about an announcement by the student activities office. The school's movie club will sell concessions on movie night each Wednesday. A variety of food and drinks will be sold. The woman objects to the selling of food and drinks for two reasons. The first is that she thinks people will be bothered by them. She mentions that the smell of popcorn might annoy people without any food. She also comments that people will make noise eating and drinking their snacks during the movie. The second reason is that she doesn't like what will happen with the money. She doesn't want the school to receive the money because tuition is already very expensive. She thinks the money should be donated to a good cause instead.

🎧 Q3_00_1

Signal Redundancy

Animals often signal others of their same species. The primary reason for doing so is to warn them of approaching danger. Animals may use visual signals, acoustic signals, or chemical signals in the form of pheromones. In some cases, animals give two or more signals at the same time. This signal redundancy increases the probability of other animals recognizing what is happening and thereby realizing that they need to flee from danger.

The professor talks about the white-tailed deer. Explain how it is related to signal redundancy.

PREPARATION TIME

00:00:30

RESPONSE TIME

00:00:60

Now listen to a lecture on this topic in a zoology class.

W Professor: The white-tailed deer is known for using a variety of signals in its daily life. Each of them serves a different purpose. Let me go over some of these signals one by one to tell you how they're used.

The most vital signal the deer gives is the one when danger, uh, like a predator, is approaching. The primary manner in which the white-tailed deer gives an alarm signal is by raising its distinctive white tail. When its tail is standing fully straight up, it indicates that there is danger. Other deer nearby notice this and flee.

But sometimes, um, all the deer in the herd don't see the raised tail. Zoologists have noticed that some white-tailed deer also stomp on the ground when a predator is close. This redundant signal serves to warn those deer that did not see the tail raised in warning. Since deer have highly sensitive hearing, there's a good chance they will hear the second warning and heed it.

Q3_00_2

The professor's lecture is about signals the white-tailed deer uses. The most important signal is when it raises its tail straight up. This tells other deer nearby that a predator is approaching. Any deer that see the signal run away. The professor then remarks that deer don't always see the signal, so some white-tailed deer give a second signal. They stomp on the ground to provide a warning. Deer have excellent hearing, so when they hear the stomping sound, the other deer flee. The two signals the white-tailed deer uses are an example of signal redundancy. This is the giving of two or more signals at the same time. By using signal redundancy, deer are increasing the chances that their warnings will be noted by the most deer possible.

A Read the following announcement by the dean of students. Try to understand what the announcement is about. After reading the announcement, complete the notes below.

Part-Time Work for Students

Students at Central University can now work part time at selected employers off campus. This new program is being run out of the office of the dean of students. So far, more than forty nearby business establishments have signed up to participate in the program. Interested students can obtain more information in room 103 in Mercy Hall. Students will be required to work a minimum of ten hours a week and must maintain a 3.0 GPA to qualify.

What Will Happen _____

Details _____

_____

B Listen to a conversation about the same topic. Be sure to take notes while you listen.
🎧 Q2_01_1

Man's Opinion _____

First Reason _____

Details _____

_____

Second Reason _____

Details _____

_____

C | **Read the question and write your response by using the information in your notes.**

> Question The man expresses his opinion about the announcement by the dean of students.
> Explain his opinion and the reasons he gives for holding that opinion.

D | **Now, say your response out loud to your partner. Don't look at your writing while you speak.**

🎧 Q2_01_3

Library to Undergo Changes

Fulton Library is undergoing some changes this summer. The library, which houses the university's engineering books, will be enlarged. This will result in the amount of space in the library doubling after it reopens. There will be more shelf space for books as well as study space for students. To make these changes, the library will be closed from June 1 to August 25. All books and journals at Fulton Library will be unavailable during this time.

The man expresses his opinion about the notice by the university library. Explain his opinion and the reasons he gives for holding that opinion.

PREPARATION TIME
00:00:30

RESPONSE TIME
00:00:60

A Read the following letter to the editor in the school newspaper. Try to understand what the letter is about. After reading the letter, complete the notes below.

Forbid Students from Having Double Majors

I have been lecturing to students at Central University for more than twenty years. During that time, I have witnessed numerous students attempt to graduate with two majors. More often than not, their grades have suffered as a result of this. I believe the school administration should forbid students from having double majors. They should only be allowed to have a single major, which they can then exclusively focus on.

Regards,

Lucy Hampton

Professor, Sociology Department

The Letter Writer's Opinion _____

Details _____

_____

B Listen to a conversation about the same topic. Be sure to take notes while you listen.

🎧 Q2_02_1

Woman's Opinion _____

First Reason _____

Details _____

_____

Second Reason _____

Details _____

_____

C Read the question and write your response by using the information in your notes.

Question The woman expresses her opinion about the letter to the editor in the school newspaper. Explain her opinion and the reasons she gives for holding that opinion.

D Now, say your response out loud to your partner. Don't look at your writing while you speak.

🎧 Q2_02_3

Waiting List Procedure to Change

When a class is overenrolled, some students are placed on the waiting list. In previous semesters, the waiting list was for students who signed up last. Starting this spring, the procedure will change. Professors will be required to check attendance and to note which students arrive late to class. Tardy students will be put on the waiting list. After two weeks, any students remaining on the waiting list will not be allowed to enroll in the class.

The woman expresses her opinion about the announcement by the Registrar's office. Explain her opinion and the reasons she gives for holding that opinion.

PREPARATION TIME
00:00:30

RESPONSE TIME
00:00:60

A Read the following announcement by the Music Department. Try to understand what the announcement is about. After reading the announcement, complete the notes below.

New Website Opens

The Music Department is pleased to announce the formation of a new webpage. This site is for students interested in creating music. Musicians and singers who play in bands can communicate with one another and exchange information on it. This will enable them to form groups and to schedule concerts on campus and in the local area. To become a part of this musical community, go to www.centraluniversitymusic.com. All students registering must input their ID number.

What Will Happen _____

Details _____

_____

B Listen to a conversation about the same topic. Be sure to take notes while you listen.

🎧 Q2_03_1

Man's Opinion _____

First Reason _____

Details _____

_____

Second Reason _____

Details _____

C | **Read the question and write your response by using the information in your notes.**

> Question The man expresses his opinion about the announcement by the Music Department. Explain his opinion and the reasons he gives for holding that opinion.

D | **Now, say your response out loud to your partner. Don't look at your writing while you speak.**

🎧 Q2_03_3

Theater Club to Have First Meeting

The school's newest club has scheduled its first meeting for this Saturday, September 9, at 6:00 PM. It will be in room 209 in West Hall. The club will focus on the theater and performing arts. The members will perform one play at the end of each semester. The weekly club meetings will be rehearsals for the performance. There will also be occasional meetings focusing on improving acting techniques. For more information, contact Marcia Snitker at 584-9320.

The woman expresses her opinion about the notice by the student activities office. Explain her opinion and the reasons she gives for holding that opinion.

PREPARATION TIME
00:00:30

RESPONSE TIME
00:00:60

A | Read the following letter to the editor in the school newspaper. Try to understand what the letter is about. After reading the letter, complete the notes below.

School Dormitories Need Improving

The dormitories at the school are shockingly bad. As a first-year student, I was highly disappointed by the quality of the dorm I reside in as well as the other dorms on campus. The facilities are old, there are cracks in the walls, and the rooms are small and poorly lit. The school ought to spend serious money renovating the dorms to make them better environments for students.

Regards,

Timothy Harris

Freshman

The Letter Writer's Opinion _____

Details _____

_____

B | Listen to a conversation about the same topic. Be sure to take notes while you listen.
🎧 Q2_04_1

Woman's Opinion _____

First Reason _____

Details _____

_____

Second Reason _____

Details _____

C | **Read the question and write your response by using the information in your notes.**

> Question The woman expresses her opinion about the letter to the editor in the school newspaper. Explain her opinion and the reasons she gives for holding that opinion.

D | **Now, say your response out loud to your partner. Don't look at your writing while you speak.**

iBT Practice Test

🎧 Q2_04_3

Get a Room at Bayside Gardens

Bayside Gardens is a brand-new apartment complex a three-minute walk from the Central University campus. There are one-, two-, and three-bedroom apartments available to rent. We have furnished and unfurnished apartments. In addition, the complex has a swimming pool and a fitness center. Show your student ID and qualify for a 10% reduction in rent. Call 483-2912 to set a time to visit the complex. You'll be glad you did.

The man expresses his opinion about the advertisement in the school newspaper. Explain his opinion and the reasons he gives for holding that opinion.

PREPARATION TIME
00:00:30

RESPONSE TIME
00:00:60

A Read the following announcement by the school administration. Try to understand what the announcement is about. After reading the announcement, complete the notes below.

Part-Time Work Rule Change

Students with part-time jobs may no longer work on campus more than twenty hours a week. In cases where students have two or more jobs, the cumulative number of hours worked may not exceed twenty. By working more than twenty hours, some students are depriving others of the opportunity to obtain employment on campus. Those students scheduled to work more than the limit will have their hours reduced by their employers at once.

What Will Happen _____

Details _____

B Listen to a conversation about the same topic. Be sure to take notes while you listen.

🎧 Q2_05_1

Woman's Opinion _____

First Reason _____

Details _____

Second Reason _____

Details _____

C | **Read the question and write your response by using the information in your notes.**

> Question The woman expresses her opinion about the announcement by the school administration. Explain her opinion and the reasons she gives for holding that opinion.

D | **Now, say your response out loud to your partner. Don't look at your writing while you speak.**

iBT Practice Test

Question 2 of 4

VOLUME

HELP

NEXT

READING TIME 00:00:45

Q2_05_3

Vending Machines to Be Removed

By order of the dean of engineering, all vending machines in Robinson Hall and Wilkins Hall will be removed. The vending machines in those two buildings primarily sell junk food. This includes sugary drinks, candy, and chocolate bars. These are negatively affecting the health of the school's engineering students. Students are encouraged to consume healthy foods and beverages for snacks in order to improve their health.

The man expresses his opinion about the announcement by the dean of engineering. Explain his opinion and the reasons he gives for holding that opinion.

PREPARATION TIME
00:00:30

RESPONSE TIME
00:00:60

A | **Read the following notice by the Buildings and Grounds Department. Try to understand what the notice is about. After reading the notice, complete the notes below.**

Bicycle Lanes on Campus to Be Removed

Starting on Friday, April 11, the bicycle lanes on campus will be removed. The entire process should take no more than two days. The lanes are seldom used by cyclists, so the school administration has decided to eliminate them. From now on, cyclists must ride their bicycles on the roads on campus. They must obey all traffic laws or will be ticketed. Any cyclist who rides on the sidewalk will be fined $100.

What Will Happen _____

Details _____

_____

B | **Listen to a conversation about the same topic. Be sure to take notes while you listen.**
🎧 Q2_06_1

Man's Opinion _____

First Reason _____

Details _____

_____

Second Reason _____

Details _____

_____

C | **Read the question and write your response by using the information in your notes.**

> Question The man expresses his opinion about the notice by the Buildings and Grounds Department. Explain his opinion and the reasons he gives for holding that opinion.

D | **Now, say your response out loud to your partner. Don't look at your writing while you speak.**

iBT Practice Test

Question 2 of 4

VOLUME

HELP

NEXT

READING TIME 00:00:45

🎧 Q2_06_3

Western Civilization Now Required Class

Students are reminded that all students must take Western Civilization 101 and 102 and receive a passing grade in both classes in order to graduate. This is a one-year-long course that should be taken in consecutive semesters. Students must receive a letter grade in these classes. No students are exempted from this policy. For more information, please contact the office of the dean of students at 795-2297.

The woman expresses her opinion about the announcement by the dean of students. Explain her opinion and the reasons she gives for holding that opinion.

PREPARATION TIME
00:00:30

RESPONSE TIME
00:00:60

A Read the following announcement by the student activities office. Try to understand what the announcement is about. After reading the announcement, complete the notes below.

Room Use Requires Fee Payment

Student clubs are permitted to use empty classrooms for meetings and other purposes. However, effective immediately, clubs must pay a fee to use a classroom. The standard fee is $50 for two hours. For each additional hour, a charge of $20 will be applied. All rooms must be rented for at least two hours. Contact Jim Lawson at 435-9048 to make a reservation or to ask questions.

What Will Happen _____

Details _____

_____

_____

B Listen to a conversation about the same topic. Be sure to take notes while you listen.

🎧 Q2_07_1

Woman's Opinion _____

First Reason _____

Details _____

_____

Second Reason _____

Details _____

_____

C | **Read the question and write your response by using the information in your notes.**

Question The woman expresses her opinion about the announcement by the student activities office. Explain her opinion and the reasons she gives for holding that opinion.

D | **Now, say your response out loud to your partner. Don't look at your writing while you speak.**

iBT Practice Test

Question 2 of 4

VOLUME

HELP

NEXT

READING TIME 00:00:45

🎧 Q2_07_3

Students to Pay Security Deposit for Rooms

All students living in a dormitory on campus must pay a security deposit before the semester begins. The deposit is $250. At the end of the school year, each dormitory room will be checked for damage. A student whose room has no damage will be refunded the entire deposit. A student whose room has suffered damage will have the cost of repairing the damage removed from the deposit. Any leftover money will be returned to the student.

The man expresses his opinion about the notice by the student housing office. Explain his opinion and the reasons he gives for holding that opinion.

PREPARATION TIME
00:00:30

RESPONSE TIME
00:00:60

A | Read the following notice by the university gym. Try to understand what the notice is about. After reading the notice, complete the notes below.

Squash Courts Available

The renovations at Carter Gymnasium are complete. The gym now has ten new squash courts. The courts are available on a first-come, first-served basis. Courts may also be reserved by calling 656-1933. Racquets may be rented at the front desk. The cost is $4 for one hour of usage. Students must show valid student ID cards to be able to use the squash courts.

What Will Happen _____

Details _____

_____

B | Listen to a conversation about the same topic. Be sure to take notes while you listen.

🎧 Q2_08_1

Man's Opinion _____

First Reason _____

Details _____

_____

Second Reason _____

Details _____

C **Read the question and write your response by using the information in your notes.**

Question The man expresses his opinion about the notice by the university gym. Explain his opinion and the reasons he gives for holding that opinion.

_____

_____

_____

_____

_____

_____

_____

_____

_____

_____

_____

_____

_____

D **Now, say your response out loud to your partner. Don't look at your writing while you speak.**

iBT Practice Test

Question 2 of 4

VOLUME

HELP

NEXT

READING TIME 00:00:45

🎧 Q2_08_3

Help Mentor Local Elementary School Students

Would you like to help a young child reach his or her full potential? Here's a great opportunity. Sign up for the new mentoring program being run by the Child Studies Department. You will meet your mentee twice a week. You can help the child with homework, play games, or just be a good friend. You won't get paid, but you will get course credit. And you might just help improve someone's life.

The woman expresses her opinion about the announcement by the Child Studies Department. Explain her opinion and the reasons she gives for holding that opinion.

PREPARATION TIME
00:00:30

RESPONSE TIME
00:00:60

A Read the following announcement by the student employment office. Try to understand what the announcement is about. After reading the announcement, complete the notes below.

Student Employee Wages to Increase

Starting on January 1, the hourly wages of all students employed on campus will increase. The rate of increase will be $2 per hour. This is being done in an effort to provide financial assistance to students working on campus. Hopefully, some students will be able to work fewer hours. This will then enable those students to spend more time on their studies.

What Will Happen _____

Details _____

_____

_____

B Listen to a conversation about the same topic. Be sure to take notes while you listen.

🎧 Q2_09_1

Woman's Opinion _____

First Reason _____

Details _____

_____

Second Reason _____

Details _____

_____

C | Read the question and write your response by using the information in your notes.

> **Question** The woman expresses her opinion about the announcement by the student employment office. Explain her opinion and the reasons she gives for holding that opinion.

_____

_____

_____

_____

_____

_____

_____

_____

_____

_____

_____

_____

_____

_____

D | Now, say your response out loud to your partner. Don't look at your writing while you speak.

🎧 Q2_09_3

Library to Remove Old Books

The main library at Central University will be disposing of approximately 5,000 books this summer. The books are all ones which have not been checked out for more than ten years. The books are being removed to increase the amount of shelf space for new books. All of the old books will be available for purchase at a later date in summer. More details will be provided next month.

The man expresses his opinion about the announcement by the university library. Explain his opinion and the reasons he gives for holding that opinion.

PREPARATION TIME
00:00:30

RESPONSE TIME
00:00:60

A Read the following notice by the university administration. Try to understand what the notice is about. After reading the notice, complete the notes below.

Faculty Parking Lot Expansion

This winter vacation, the faculty parking lot behind Walker Hall will be expanded. The lot currently has space for 150 vehicles. Following the expansion, the lot will have space for 220 vehicles. This should enable a majority of faculty members to park their cars near their classrooms. The picnic area behind Walker Hall will be removed to make room for the expansion. More information can be obtained by visiting room 405 in Hampton Hall.

What Will Happen _____

Details _____

_____

_____

B Listen to a conversation about the same topic. Be sure to take notes while you listen.

🎧 Q2_10_1

Woman's Opinion _____

First Reason _____

Details _____

_____

Second Reason _____

Details _____

_____

C | Read the question and write your response by using the information in your notes.

> Question The woman expresses her opinion about the notice by the university administration. Explain her opinion and the reasons she gives for holding that opinion.

D | Now, say your response out loud to your partner. Don't look at your writing while you speak.

iBT Practice Test

Question 2 of 4

VOLUME

HELP

NEXT

READING TIME 00:00:45

🎧 Q2_10_3

Not Enough Places to Study

There are not enough places for students to study in the library at night. I therefore propose that the school keep the classrooms on campus unlocked until 2:00 A.M. every day of the week. That way, students can have their own private places to study. Studying in quiet places such as empty classrooms will enable students to improve their knowledge and to learn better.

Anthony Garner
Sophomore

The woman expresses her opinion about the letter to the editor in the school newspaper. Explain her opinion and the reasons she gives for holding that opinion.

PREPARATION TIME
00:00:30

RESPONSE TIME
00:00:60

A | Read the following passage. Try to understand what the passage is about. After reading the passage, complete the notes below.

Evolution in Action

The process through which living organisms adapt over time to become better able to survive is known as evolution. In general, it takes multiple generations to occur, so it is not easily observed. However, in some rare cases, evolution takes place quickly, which allows scientists to study it. This evolution in action is crucial to scientists because it permits them to understand how species adapt to survive in a rapid manner.

Main Idea of the Passage _____

Details _____

_____

B | Listen to a lecture about the same topic. Be sure to take notes while you listen. 🎧 Q3_01_1

Thesis Statement _____

First Example _____

Details _____

_____

Second Example _____

Details _____

_____

C | **Read the question and write your response by using the information in your notes.**

Question The professor talks about the cane toad and the peppered moth. Explain how they are related to evolution in action.

_____

_____

_____

_____

_____

_____

_____

_____

_____

_____

_____

_____

D | **Now, say your response out loud to your partner. Don't look at your writing while you speak.**

iBT Practice Test

Question 3 of 4

VOLUME

HELP

NEXT

READING TIME 00:00:45

🎧 Q3_01_3

False Animal Alarm Calls

Animals make alarm calls to warn others of approaching predators. The sounds they make alert other animals nearby of danger, allowing them to hide or flee. There are some animals which make false alarm calls. They make sounds despite no predators being around, so other animals flee. This leaves the animal that made the false call all alone. Typically, it takes advantage of this situation by consuming the food the others were eating.

The professor talks about the African fork-tailed drongo. Explain how its actions are related to false animal alarm calls.

PREPARATION TIME
00:00:30

RESPONSE TIME
00:00:60

A | **Read the following passage. Try to understand what the passage is about. After reading the passage, complete the notes below.**

The You-Too Fallacy

People often respond to others criticizing them by saying, "You, too." A person using this argument essentially states that the accuser is guilty of doing the same thing. The person thereby asserts that he or she is doing nothing wrong. For instance, a person accused of lying may respond, "You, too," meaning that the accuser also lies, so lying is not bad. This is a logical fallacy because the accuser's behavior does not excuse the actions of the other person.

Main Idea of the Passage _____

Details _____

_____

B | **Listen to a lecture about the same topic. Be sure to take notes while you listen.** 🎧 Q3_02_1

Thesis Statement _____

Example _____

What the Professor's Brother Does _____

_____

What the Professor Does _____

_____

C | **Read the question and write your response by using the information in your notes.**

> Question The professor talks about his relationship with his older brother. Explain how it is related to the you-too fallacy.

D | **Now, say your response out loud to your partner. Don't look at your writing while you speak.**

🎧 Q3_02_3

Implicit Memory

People do various actions without having to take the time to remember how to do them. Instead, they unconsciously remember the steps required to do these actions. This is implicit memory. It is used to recall actions common for most people. These include physical acts as well as household chores. The steps involved are ingrained in people's minds, so they do not consciously need to think about how to do them.

The professor talks about common physical activities. Explain how they are related to implicit memory.

PREPARATION TIME
00:00:30

RESPONSE TIME
00:00:60

A Read the following passage. Try to understand what the passage is about. After reading the passage, complete the notes below.

Reward Power

Employers frequently motivate their employees by offering them rewards. Managers and executives possess this reward power at business establishments. The rewards may be tangible or intangible. Tangible ones include money, such as salary increases and bonuses, as well as plaques, certificates, and awards. Intangible awards are comprised of praise, recognition, and positive feedback. Rewards of any form are appreciated by hardworking employees, who enjoy being acknowledged for the work they do.

Main Idea of the Passage _____

Details _____

_____

_____

_____

B Listen to a lecture about the same topic. Be sure to take notes while you listen. 🎧 Q3_03_1

Example _____

Details _____

_____

_____

_____

Results _____

Details _____

_____

_____

C | **Read the question and write your response by using the information in your notes.**

Question The professor talks about his old college roommate. Explain how her actions are related to reward power.

D | **Now, say your response out loud to your partner. Don't look at your writing while you speak.**

🎧 Q3_03_3

Giffen Goods

In most cases, when a product's price increases, the demand for it decreases. This is not the case for Giffen goods though. Named after noted nineteenth-century economist Robert Giffen, when the price of a Giffen good goes up, demand for it increases. Giffen goods are rare and can be all kinds of products. However, in most cases, they are staples that nothing else can replace.

The professor talks about the Irish potato famine. Explain how it is related to Giffen goods.

PREPARATION TIME
00:00:30

RESPONSE TIME
00:00:60

A | Read the following passage. Try to understand what the passage is about. After reading the passage, complete the notes below.

Subject Expectancy Effect

During scientific and medical experiments with human subjects, there is a tendency for the people involved to have certain expectations regarding the outcomes of them. This can sometimes cause the results of experiments to be altered. The subjects may engage in this subject expectancy effect either consciously or unconsciously. Because they have a preconceived idea of what the results should be, they skew the results toward their expectations.

Main Idea of the Passage _____

Details _____

_____

B | Listen to a lecture about the same topic. Be sure to take notes while you listen. 🎧 Q3_04_1

Example _____

What Happened _____

Details _____

_____

_____

How the Professor Solved the Problem _____

Details _____

_____

C | **Read the question and write your response by using the information in your notes.**

Question The professor talks about his experience at a pharmaceutical company. Explain how it is related to the subject expectancy effect.

D | **Now, say your response out loud to your partner. Don't look at your writing while you speak.**

🎧 Q3_04_3

Passive Attention

Some people are able to concentrate passively, especially if the activity they are doing is more static than dynamic. By using passive attention, a person can observe an activity without expending much effort. There are both advantages and disadvantages to doing this. Passive attention can help the mind rest and induces a state of relaxation. However, it can result in a lack of understanding of a situation if close attention is required.

The professor talks about static situations. Explain how they are related to passive attention.

PREPARATION TIME
00:00:30

RESPONSE TIME
00:00:60

A | Read the following passage. Try to understand what the passage is about. After reading the passage, complete the notes below.

Product Licensing

Making and selling new products is often difficult. Thus, people with good ideas for new products tend to license them to existing companies. In doing so, they sell the rights to their products to these businesses. There are several advantages to this. The businesses take on the burden and cost of producing and advertising the products. In addition, the creators receive royalties in the form of a percentage of the sales of their products.

Main Idea of the Passage _____

Details _____

_____

_____

B | Listen to a lecture about the same topic. Be sure to take notes while you listen. 🎧 Q3_05_1

Thesis Statement _____

Example _____

Details _____

_____

What Happened Afterward _____

Details _____

_____

C | **Read the question and write your response by using the information in your notes.**

Question The professor talks about the invention of a refrigerator motor. Explain how it is related to product licensing.

D | **Now, say your response out loud to your partner. Don't look at your writing while you speak.**

🎧 Q3_05_3

Ambient Advertising

In recent times, unusual advertisements are being placed in unexpected places more frequently. This is ambient advertising. The objective is to attract attention to the ads by making them very eye catching. Ambient advertising tends to be effective since it may surprise and delight potential customers. This results in them both thinking about the product and discussing it with others. This, in turn, enables news of the product to spread by word of mouth.

The professor talks about some advertisements he recently saw. Explain how they are related to ambient advertising.

PREPARATION TIME
00:00:30

RESPONSE TIME
00:00:60

A Read the following passage. Try to understand what the passage is about. After reading the passage, complete the notes below.

Animal Regeneration

Some animals are capable of regenerating body parts. When a body part, such as a tail or leg, is lost or cut off, the animal's body can grow a new part. In some cases, the new body part looks exactly like the one that it replaced. In other cases, the new body part may be smaller or somehow look different than the old part. The regenerated body parts are able to function just like the original ones.

Main Idea of the Passage _____

Details _____

_____

_____

B Listen to a lecture about the same topic. Be sure to take notes while you listen. 🎧 Q3_06_1

First Example _____

Details _____

_____

_____

Second Example _____

Details _____

_____

_____

C | **Read the question and write your response by using the information in your notes.**

Question The professor talks about starfish and spiders. Explain how they are related to animal regeneration.

D | **Now, say your response out loud to your partner. Don't look at your writing while you speak.**

🎧 Q3_06_3

Hydrothermal Vents

In some places in the world's oceans, there are hydrothermal vents. They normally form near underwater volcanoes and in places where the Earth's plates are drifting apart. They are essentially underwater fountains. They shoot hot water filled with various minerals into the ocean. Many hydrothermal vents have their own microecosystems. So marine animals live around them even though the vents may be located thousands of meters beneath the surface.

The professor talks about black smokers. Explain how they are related to hydrothermal vents.

PREPARATION TIME
00:00:30

RESPONSE TIME
00:00:60

A Read the following passage. Try to understand what the passage is about. After reading the passage, complete the notes below.

Delegating Authority

In the business world, managers are often unable to control everything happening in their departments or spheres of influence. They must therefore transfer power, or authority, to others. This is the process known as delegating authority. When delegating authority, a manager gives another employee—often one of lower status—the power to make decisions regarding certain matters. This enables companies to operate more efficiently. It also gives employees more experience since it lets them be involved in decision-making processes.

Main Idea of the Passage _____

Details _____

_____

_____

B Listen to a lecture about the same topic. Be sure to take notes while you listen. 🎧 Q3_07_1

Thesis Statement _____

What the Professor Did at First _____

Details _____

_____

_____

What the Professor Did Later _____

Details _____

_____

_____

C | **Read the question and write your response by using the information in your notes.**

> Question The professor talks about his experience owning a company. Explain how it is related to delegating authority.

_____

_____

_____

_____

_____

_____

_____

_____

_____

_____

_____

_____

_____

D | **Now, say your response out loud to your partner. Don't look at your writing while you speak.**

Q3_07_3

Mere Deadline Effect

Most company workers have multiple tasks to complete. They must prioritize them in order to decide which tasks to complete first. Most people focus on the tasks that are time sensitive over the tasks that do not have impending deadlines. They do this even when the tasks that are not time sensitive are of greater importance or could yield better results. Instead, they complete those tasks with urgent deadlines first. This is the mere deadline effect.

The professor talks about her college roommate. Explain how her actions are related to the mere deadline effect.

PREPARATION TIME
00:00:30

RESPONSE TIME
00:00:60

A | Read the following passage. Try to understand what the passage is about. After reading the passage, complete the notes below.

Anxiety

Almost everybody suffers from stress at various times. Stress can be caused by a variety of factors. These include work, school, and personal relationships. The body's natural response to any kind of stress is anxiety. Anxiety refers to feelings of fear, concern, or worry about something that is happening or that will happen. In some cases, these feelings may last a long time, which may result in anxiety disorder.

Main Idea of the Passage _____

Details _____

_____

_____

_____

B | Listen to a lecture about the same topic. Be sure to take notes while you listen. 🎧 Q3_08_1

Thesis Statement _____

What Happened _____

Details _____

_____

_____

_____

_____

C | Read the question and write your response by using the information in your notes.

> Question The professor talks about his experience as a student. Explain how it is related to anxiety.

D | Now, say your response out loud to your partner. Don't look at your writing while you speak.

🎧 Q3_08_3

Teamwork

Teamwork is a cooperative effort involving two or more individuals. Everyone in a group—or on a team—works together to achieve a shared goal. Teamwork allows all of the individuals in a group to focus on their strengths while avoiding their weaknesses. Ideally, this lets the group accomplish its goal quickly and efficiently. Teamwork is practiced in sports and at homes, schools, and workplaces.

The professor talks about group projects. Explain how they are related to teamwork.

PREPARATION TIME
00:00:30

RESPONSE TIME
00:00:60

A **Read the following passage. Try to understand what the passage is about. After reading the passage, complete the notes below.**

Droughts

Some regions experience times with below-average amounts of precipitation. When this condition lasts for weeks, months, or even years, there is a drought. A drought can have a wide range of effects. It can cause water levels in lakes, rivers, and streams to become lower. It can reduce the amount of moisture in the soil and deplete groundwater supplies. It can also damage crops and harm people because of a lack of water for farming and drinking.

Main Idea of the Passage _____

Details _____

_____

_____

B **Listen to a lecture about the same topic. Be sure to take notes while you listen.** 🎧 Q3_09_1

Thesis Statement _____

First Example _____

Details _____

_____

_____

Second Example _____

Details _____

_____

C | Read the question and write your response by using the information in your notes.

Question The professor talks about the Mayan Empire and the Old Kingdom in Egypt. Explain how they are related to droughts.

D | Now, say your response out loud to your partner. Don't look at your writing while you speak.

🎧 Q3_09_3

Water Erosion

Water erosion refers to the removal or displacement of the ground due to the actions of water. In many cases, valuable topsoil is washed away. Water erosion can happen gradually. An example is the formation of the Grand Canyon by the Colorado River over a period of millions of years. It can also happen quickly. This may be caused by floods from seasonal rains, hurricanes, and typhoons. Water erosion that happens quickly can cause dramatic changes to the land.

The professor talks about the Outer Banks. Explain how it is related to water erosion.

PREPARATION TIME
00:00:30

RESPONSE TIME
00:00:60

A | Read the following passage. Try to understand what the passage is about. After reading the passage, complete the notes below.

Buoyancy

Ships, boats, rafts, and other structures can float on water thanks to a phenomenon called buoyancy. When an object is placed in the water, it displaces, or moves, a certain amount of water. If the weight of the displaced water is more than the weight of the object, such as a ship, then the object will float. This is buoyancy. Buoyancy lets ships made of objects that do not normally float, including metal, avoid sinking.

Main Idea of the Passage _____

Details _____

_____

_____

B | Listen to a lecture about the same topic. Be sure to take notes while you listen. 🎧 Q3_10_1

Thesis Statement _____

How Submarines Descend

Details _____

_____

_____

How Submarines Rise

Details _____

_____

_____

C | Read the question and write your response by using the information in your notes.

> Question The professor talks about submarines. Explain how they are related to buoyancy.

D | Now, say your response out loud to your partner. Don't look at your writing while you speak.

🎧 Q3_10_3

Magnetic Levitation

Levitation is a process that causes something to be suspended in the air. This act of defying gravity can be accomplished with magnets. Magnetic forces can counter the effects of gravity. An object can therefore be made to hover, or levitate, in the air. Multiple magnets must be used not only to suspend the object but also to keep it stable. This prevents it from falling over. There are a number of uses of magnetic levitation, including in transportation.

The professor talks about maglev trains. Explain how they are related to magnetic levitation.

PREPARATION TIME
00:00:30

RESPONSE TIME
00:00:60

Part C

Integrated Speaking Task
Listening and Speaking

Question 4

Integrated Speaking Task | Listening and Speaking

◢ About the Task

The last questions presents only a listening passage—a lecture—and not a reading passage. Test takers need to respond based on what they heard. They are given 20 seconds to prepare their response and 60 seconds to speak.

For **Question 4**, test takers will listen to a lecture about an academic topic. As in Question 4, topics for this question can be drawn from a variety of fields, including life science, social science, physical science, and the humanities. Again, no prior knowledge is necessary to understand the lecture. After hearing the lecture, test takers are asked to summarize the lecture and to explain how the examples are connected with the overall topic.

When you answer this question, be sure to focus on what the professor discusses. All of the information you discuss should come from the professor's talk. Even if you possess outside knowledge of the topic, you should not use it. Instead, focus solely on the information that the professor provides and then explain how it relates to the question.

🎧 Q4_00_1

Using points and examples from the talk, explain two ways that people can overcome plant seed dormancy.

PREPARATION TIME
00:00:20

RESPONSE TIME
00:00:60

Listen to part of a lecture in a botany class.

W Professor: Plant seed dormancy is an embryonic state in which seeds do not germinate. You see, uh, many plant seeds simply won't germinate unless the right conditions exist. There are, however, a couple of ways we can overcome the tendency of seeds to remain dormant.

Let me use the red oak tree as my first example. Its seeds are acorns which only germinate in cold, moist conditions, uh, like on a forest floor in winter. Here's how we can get these seeds to overcome their dormancy . . . First, place the acorns in a cool environment such as a refrigerator. The acorns need to be in transparent plastic bags. They should also be kept moist. The temperature needs to be between two and five degrees Celsius. If you keep them in cold storage like that, the red oak tree seeds will germinate in around thirty days.

Another way to get plant seeds to end their dormant period is to remove their outer shells. This can be done with the black locust tree seed, which has a hard shell. In natural conditions, around ten percent of the black locust tree's seeds germinate. Now, uh, to remove the shells, pour very hot water over the seeds in a container. Do this a few times to make the shells soft. Then, carefully remove the shells with a knife, being sure not to damage the inner seeds. Plant those seeds, and they'll quickly germinate.

The professor lectures to the class on plant seed dormancy. She states that some seeds won't germinate except under the proper conditions. She then gives two examples of how to overcome plant seed dormancy. The first involves the red oak tree, which has acorns for seeds. She says that the tree's acorns only germinate in cold conditions. She recommends making the acorns moist and then putting them in a refrigerator for a month. According to her, the seeds will germinate if a person does that. Next, she discusses the black locust tree. Its seeds are in hard shells, so a person should pour hot water over them a few times. Next, the person should take the seeds out of their shells and plant them to make them germinate.

A Listen to a lecture on zoology. Be sure to take notes while you listen. 🎧 Q4_01_1

Main Topic _____

Main Idea _____

First Advantage _____

Details _____

_____

_____

_____

_____

Second Advantage _____

Details _____

_____

_____

_____

_____

B | **Read the question and write your response by using the information in your notes.**

Question Using points and examples from the talk, explain two advantages of young female rhesus monkeys taking care of newborn monkeys.

_____

_____

_____

_____

_____

_____

_____

_____

_____

_____

_____

_____

_____

C | **Now, say your response out loud to your partner. Don't look at your writing while you speak.**

🎧 Q4_01_3

Using points and examples from the talk, explain how the giraffe has evolved to gain advantages while eating.

PREPARATION TIME
00:00:20

RESPONSE TIME
00:00:60

A | **Listen to a lecture on economics. Be sure to take notes while you listen.** 🎧 Q4_02_1

Main Topic _____

Main Idea _____

First Way _____

Details _____

_____

_____

_____

Second Way _____

Details _____

_____

_____

_____

_____

B Read the question and write your response by using the information in your notes.

> Question Using points and examples from the talk, explain how businesses can build rapport with their clients.

C Now, say your response out loud to your partner. Don't look at your writing while you speak.

🎧 Q4_02_3

Using points and examples from the talk, explain two types of investments that companies make.

PREPARATION TIME
00:00:20

RESPONSE TIME
00:00:60

A | **Listen to a lecture on psychology. Be sure to take notes while you listen.** 🎧 Q4_03_1

Main Topic _____

Main Idea _____

First Example _____

Details _____

_____

_____

_____

_____

Second Example _____

Details _____

_____

_____

_____

B | **Read the question and write your response by using the information in your notes.**

Question Using points and examples from the talk, explain how excessive planning can often lead to problems.

_____

_____

_____

_____

_____

_____

_____

_____

_____

_____

_____

_____

_____

C | **Now, say your response out loud to your partner. Don't look at your writing while you speak.**

🎧 Q4_03_3

Using points and examples from the talk, explain two ways that people motivate themselves.

PREPARATION TIME
00:00:20

RESPONSE TIME
00:00:60

A | **Listen to a lecture on meteorology. Be sure to take notes while you listen.** 🎧 Q4_04_1

Main Topic _____

Main Idea _____

First Type _____

Details _____

_____

_____

_____

_____

Second Type _____

Details _____

_____

_____

_____

_____

B | **Read the question and write your response by using the information in your notes.**

> Question Using points and examples from the talk, explain how two different types of ice formations are created.

_____

_____

_____

_____

_____

_____

_____

_____

_____

_____

_____

_____

_____

C | **Now, say your response out loud to your partner. Don't look at your writing while you speak.**

🎧 Q4_04_3

Using points and examples from the talk, explain how sand dunes make singing sounds.

PREPARATION TIME
00 : 00 : 20

RESPONSE TIME
00 : 00 : 60

A | **Listen to a lecture on anthropology. Be sure to take notes while you listen.** 🎧 Q4_05_1

Main Topic

Main Idea

First Benefit

Details

Second Benefit

Details

B | **Read the question and write your response by using the information in your notes.**

Question Using points and examples from the talk, explain how fire helped early humans.

_____

_____

_____

_____

_____

_____

_____

_____

_____

_____

_____

_____

C | **Now, say your response out loud to your partner. Don't look at your writing while you speak.**

🎧 Q4_05_3

Using points and examples from the talk, explain how primary demand and secondary demand influence advertising.

PREPARATION TIME
00:00:20

RESPONSE TIME
00:00:60

A | **Listen to a lecture on sociology. Be sure to take notes while you listen.** 🎧 Q4_06_1

Main Topic _____

Main Idea _____

First Benefit _____

Details _____

_____

_____

_____

_____

Second Benefit _____

Details _____

_____

_____

_____

_____

B | Read the question and write your response by using the information in your notes.

> Question Using points and examples from the talk, explain two benefits of toll roads.

_____

_____

_____

_____

_____

_____

_____

_____

_____

_____

_____

_____

_____

C | Now, say your response out loud to your partner. Don't look at your writing while you speak.

Q4_06_3

Using points and examples from the talk, explain two reasons that the professor opposes public financing of sports stadiums.

PREPARATION TIME
00:00:20

RESPONSE TIME
00:00:60

A | **Listen to a lecture on zoology. Be sure to take notes while you listen.** 🎧 Q4_07_1

Main Topic _____

Main Idea _____

First Example _____

Details _____

_____

_____

_____

_____

Second Example _____

Details _____

_____

_____

_____

_____

B | **Read the question and write your response by using the information in your notes.**

Question Using points and examples from the talk, explain how the thorny devil lizard and the Mojave Desert tortoise get water.

_____

_____

_____

_____

_____

_____

_____

_____

_____

_____

_____

_____

_____

C | **Now, say your response out loud to your partner. Don't look at your writing while you speak.**

Q4_07_3

Using points and examples from the talk, explain how carpenter ants and weaver ants make nests.

PREPARATION TIME
00:00:20

RESPONSE TIME
00:00:60

A | **Listen to a lecture on marketing. Be sure to take notes while you listen.** 🎧 Q4_08_1

Main Topic _____

Main Idea _____

First Drawback _____

Details _____

_____

_____

_____

_____

Second Drawback _____

Details _____

_____

_____

_____

_____

B   **Read the question and write your response by using the information in your notes.**

> Question Using points and examples from the talk, explain two drawbacks for companies using celebrity endorsements.

C   **Now, say your response out loud to your partner. Don't look at your writing while you speak.**

🎧 Q4_08_3

Using points and examples from the talk, explain two ways that companies can build brand equity.

PREPARATION TIME
00 : 00 : 20

RESPONSE TIME
00 : 00 : 60

A | **Listen to a lecture on zoology. Be sure to take notes while you listen.** 🎧 Q4_09_1

Main Topic _____

Main Idea _____

First Reason _____

Details _____

_____

_____

_____

_____

Second Reason _____

Details _____

_____

_____

_____

_____

B | **Read the question and write your response by using the information in your notes.**

> Question Using points and examples from the talk, explain why the dragonfly is such an effective hunter.

C | **Now, say your response out loud to your partner. Don't look at your writing while you speak.**

🎧 Q4_09_3

Using points and examples from the talk, explain how the spotted hyena and the bottlenose dolphin reconcile after fights.

PREPARATION TIME
00:00:20

RESPONSE TIME
00:00:60

A | **Listen to a lecture on archaeology. Be sure to take notes while you listen.** 🎧 Q4_10_1

Main Topic _____

Main Idea _____

First Way _____

Details _____

_____

_____

_____

_____

Second Way _____

Details _____

_____

_____

_____

_____

B | Read the question and write your response by using the information in your notes.

> Question Using points and examples from the talk, explain two ways that archaeological dig sites can be harmed.

C | Now, say your response out loud to your partner. Don't look at your writing while you speak.

Q4_10_3

Using points and examples from the talk, explain the different features of Hadrian's Wall.

PREPARATION TIME
00:00:20

RESPONSE TIME
00:00:60

Actual Test

AT00

Speaking Section Directions

 Make sure your headset is on.

This section measures your ability to speak about a variety of topics. You will answer four questions by speaking into the microphone. Answer as completely as possible.

In the first question, you will speak about familiar topics. Your response will be scored on your ability to speak clearly and coherently.

In the next two questions, you will first read a short reading passage. This passage will go away, and you will then listen to a talk on the same topic. You will be asked about the information you have read and heard. You will need to combine information from the reading passage and the talk to provide a complete answer. Your response will be scored on your ability to speak clearly and coherently and how accurately you convey information about what you read and heard.

In the last question, you will listen to part of a lecture. You will be asked about what you have heard. Your response will be scored on your ability to speak clearly and coherently and how accurately you convey information about what you heard.

You may take notes while you read and while you listen to the conversations and lectures. You may use your notes to help prepare your response.

Listen carefully to the directions for each question. The directions will not be written on the screen.

For each question, you will be given a short time to prepare your response (15 to 30 seconds, depending on the question). A clock will show how much preparation time is remaining. When the preparation time is up, you will be told to begin your response. A clock will show how much response time is remaining. A message will appear on the screen when the response time has ended.

🎧 AT01

Do you agree or disagree with the following statement?

It is possible to be good friends with someone who has different opinions than you.

Please include specific examples and details to support your explanation.

PREPARATION TIME
00:00:15

RESPONSE TIME
00:00:45

AT02

University Flea Market Needed

I have noticed that many students throw away perfectly good items all throughout the school year. This is especially true at the end of the spring and fall terms. I have seen couches, televisions, refrigerators, and other items thrown away. This is wasteful. I suggest that the school hold a flea market at the conclusion of each semester. That way, students can sell unwanted items while others can purchase items they need for the coming term.

Regards,

Lance Jarvis
Junior

The man expresses his opinion about the letter to the editor in the school newspaper. Explain his opinion and the reasons he gives for holding that opinion.

PREPARATION TIME
00:00:30

RESPONSE TIME
00:00:60

🎧 AT03

Stratification

As sedimentary and igneous rocks are created, they often form in layers. The layers may be thin sheets a few millimeters thick. Or they may be several meters thick. The layers are created due to different conditions when the rocks form. This process is known as stratification. When several layers of rocks are exposed, it is easy to see the stratification of rocks in a certain area. Individual layers of rocks may vary in color, texture, and composition.

The professor talks about the Badlands. Explain how it is related to stratification.

PREPARATION TIME
00:00:30

RESPONSE TIME
00:00:60

🎧 AT04

Using points and examples from the talk, explain why some plants do not lean toward the sun.

PREPARATION TIME
00:00:20

RESPONSE TIME
00:00:60

Authors

Michael A. Putlack
- MA in History, Tufts University, Medford, MA, USA
- Expert test developer of TOEFL, TOEIC, and TEPS
- Main author of the Darakwon *How to Master Skills for the TOEFL® iBT* series and *TOEFL® MAP* series

Stephen Poirier
- Candidate for PhD in History, University of Western Ontario, Canada
- Certificate of Professional Technical Writing, Carleton University, Canada
- Co-author of the Darakwon *How to Master Skills for the TOEFL® iBT* series and *TOEFL® MAP* series

Tony Covello
- BA in Political Science, Beloit College, Beloit, WI, USA
- MA in TEFL, International Graduate School of English, Seoul, Korea
- Term instructor at George Mason University Korea, Songdo, Incheon, Korea

Decoding the TOEFL® iBT
SPEAKING Intermediate NEW TOEFL® EDITION

Publisher Chung Kyudo
Editor Kim Minju
Authors Michael A. Putlack, Stephen Poirier, Tony Covello
Proofreader Michael A. Putlack
Designers Koo Soojung, Park Sunyoung

First published in September 2021
By Darakwon, Inc.
Darakwon Bldg., 211, Munbal-ro, Paju-si, Gyeonggi-do 10881
Republic of Korea
Tel: 82-2-736-2031 (Ext. 250)
Fax: 82-2-732-2037

ISBN 978-89-277-0002-7 14740
978-89-277-0875-9 14740 (set)

www.darakwon.co.kr

Components Student Book / Answer Book
8 7 6 5 4 3 2   24 25 26 27 28

Decoding the TOEFL® iBT

Scripts & Sample Answers

Intermediate

SPEAKING

Decoding the
TOEFL® iBT

Intermediate

SPEAKING Scripts &
Sample Answers

Question 1 #1 — p. 14

A

Having Dinner with Family Members

I understand why people want to have dinner with their friends. However, I would prefer to eat with my family members. For one thing, we always eat at home, and my mother is an excellent cook. She makes delicious meals at home, so I know I will have a great dinner by eating with my family. Next, I enjoy being with my family members. When we eat together, we talk about our day. We tell one another what we did, and we also discuss our future plans. Just last night, while we ate, we had a talk about our upcoming summer trip. So our dinner conversations are entertaining as well.

Having Dinner with Friends

Of the two choices, I would rather have dinner with my friends. The first reason is that my friends and I enjoy cooking together. It's our hobby, so we have a great time working together in the kitchen. Everyone helps prepare the meal, and then we get to taste the results of our hard work. Last weekend, five of us cooked a fancy Italian dinner and loved it. The second reason is that after dinner is over, we like doing something together. For example, last week, we went to a theater to see a movie. The next time, we intend to visit the park to walk by the river.

iBT Practice Test

Sample Outline 1

Attend University after Graduating

1 **maintain studying mindset**
   - brother went straight to university → no problems
   - sister took 2 years off → couldn't focus on school

2 **best to get studying done soon**
   - graduate in early 20s
   - begin career at early age

Sample Response 1 🎧 Q1_01_4

Attend University after Graduating

In my opinion, it's a good idea to attend university immediately after graduating from high school. First, by going to university then, you can maintain the studying mindset. My brother went straight to university after graduating, and he had no problems studying hard. But my sister took two years off. She said she had trouble focusing on her studies when she went back to school. Second, it's best to get all of one's studying done as soon as possible. If you go straight to university after high school, you can graduate in your early twenties. After that, you can begin your career at an early age. That will help you in the long term.

Sample Outline 2

Take Time off before Attending University

1 **brother took time off**
   - saved money for school
   - paid tuition w/saved money = didn't borrow money

2 **brother was more mature**
   - other students didn't study hard
   - brother had good work ethic → got highest grades

Sample Response 2 🎧 Q1_01_5

Take Time off before Attending University

It would be better to take some time off before attending university than to go there right after finishing high school. When my brother finished high school, he got a job and worked for three years. That let him save money for school. When he enrolled at his university, he paid for his tuition with the money he had saved. Thus, he didn't have to borrow any money to attend school. He also said that he was much more mature than the other students. They didn't study hard, but he had developed a good work ethic while he was employed. So he almost always got the highest grade in each of his classes.

Question 1 #2 — p. 17

A

Agree

Nowadays, there are countless programs on television with excessive violence and bad language. I believe the government should regulate those shows. First off, many children accidentally turn the channel to these shows and wind up watching them. Children shouldn't be exposed to that kind of adult content. Once when I was young, I watched a show with bad language by accident. My parents were so upset about that. Furthermore, shows with excessive violence and language are bad influences on people, especially teenagers. For example, teenagers often imitate the things they see on television, so they develop poor morals. I don't want that to happen, so these shows need to be regulated.

Disagree

I don't think the government should regulate any television programs. To begin with, people have the right to choose what they want to do. The government has no right to tell people what they should or should not watch. If people want to watch movies with lots of violence and bad language, they should be allowed to do so. In addition, I understand that parents don't want their children exposed to these programs. But it's their job as parents to monitor what their children are watching. My parents made sure that my sister and I didn't watch any bad shows. They didn't need the government to help them.

iBT Practice Test

Sample Outline 1

Agree

1 **father's boss is friends w/employees**
   - hangs out w/employees after work
   - employees love working for him → work harder

2 **work environment = better**
   - workers at father's company rarely get in arguments
   - help others → thanks to positive work environment

Sample Response 1 ∩ Q1_02_4

Agree

I agree with the statement one hundred percent. My father works at a small company. His boss is good friends with many of the employees, including my father. He hangs out with the employees after work and socializes with them. As a result, the employees all love working for him. They work much harder than employees who dislike their boss do. In addition, when bosses and workers are close, the working environment is much better. People at my father's company rarely get into arguments. They also help one another constantly. This is a result of the positive work environment created by the relationship between the boss and the employees.

Sample Outline 2

Disagree

1 **difference between boss and workers**
   - being close = strange
   - mom doesn't want to be friends w/supervisor

2 **people tell friends about work problems**
   - can't do that w/boss
   - awkward + poor work environment

Sample Response 2 ∩ Q1_02_5

Disagree

Bosses and workers being close doesn't sound like a good idea to me. I therefore disagree with the statement. First, there is a distinct difference between a boss and the people who work for the boss. So it would be strange for them to be close to one another. My mother doesn't want to be friends with her supervisor. She thinks it's not even possible because of their work relationship. Something else to consider is that people normally tell their friends about their problems. These include work problems. However, there's no way that employees could complain about their jobs to their bosses. That would be awkward and would create a poor work environment.

Question 1 #3   p. 20

A

Staying at Home

When I was young, I always preferred to stay at home on the weekend. First, I got the opportunity to spend time with my parents. Both of my parents worked, so they couldn't do many activities with me on weekdays. Consequently, on weekends, my parents and I always spent time together. That allowed me to become close to my parents. Another thing is that when I was young, I loved playing computer games. My parents bought me a computer, and they permitted me to play computer games for an hour or two on the weekend. That was also a fun activity which I could only do at my home.

Visiting a Relative's House

There was nothing better than visiting a relative's house on the weekend when I was young. My grandparents lived an hour away from us, so we frequently drove to their home. They had all kinds of toys for my brothers and me. My grandmother also always cooked delicious food for us. I have very fond memories of visiting their house as a child. We used to go to my uncle's home, too. He has two sons, so my brothers, cousins, and I would go to the park and play sports. We played basketball and soccer for several hours each day. Those were some of the best times in my life.

iBT Practice Test

Sample Outline 1

Having My Own Business

1 **make all decision**
   - am leader, not follower

- want to be in charge of group

2 **everything = my responsibility**
   - like the challenge
   - success or failure of company up to me → pressure to do best

Sample Response 1 🎧 Q1_03_4

Having My Own Business

In my opinion, it would be better to have my own business than to work for another person. First, by having my own business, I could make all of the decisions. I think of myself as a leader, not a follower. I prefer to be in charge of every group I belong to. Therefore, in the future, I want to have my own business so that I can be the leader. Second, if I'm the owner of the company, everything that happens is my responsibility. I like that kind of challenge. Whether my company succeeds or fails is up to me. That kind of pressure will encourage me to do my best.

Sample Outline 2

Working for Another Person

1 **uncle has own business**
   - very stressful → worries about company every day
   - no days off → stress
   - don't want to live like that

2 **better at following orders than giving them**
   - hate leading groups at school
   - excellent at following directions = will be great employee

Sample Response 2 🎧 Q1_03_5

Working for Another Person

I would prefer to work for another person than to have my own business. My uncle has his own business, and it's extremely stressful for him. He has to worry about the condition of his company every day. He never gets a day off either, so his life is full of stress. I don't want to live that way, so I would prefer to work for someone else. As for me, I'm much better at following orders than at giving them. I hate leading groups at school, but I'm excellent at following the team leader's directions. I'm positive that I'll make a great employee in the future.

A

Agree

I think teachers should give their students lots of assignments, so I agree with the statement. First of all, teachers have to confirm that their students understand the material being taught. The best way to do this is to give students homework. When teachers check homework, they can find out if the students know the material or don't understand it. Then, they can either move on to new material or go over the old material again. Next, assignments are a great way for students to improve their knowledge. I must often do research to complete my school assignments. When doing that, I learn more and therefore become more knowledgeable.

Disagree

Most people might agree with this statement, but I disagree with it. To begin with, students these days are overworked. I have between three and four hours of homework every day. If all of my teachers give many assignments, then I'll become even busier. I probably won't even have enough time to finish my homework every day. Another thing to consider is that a great deal of homework is merely busy work. For instance, math teachers love assigning problems for students to solve. But if the students understand the material, there's no need for them to do twenty or thirty problems. Solving ten problems is more than enough.

iBT Practice Test

Sample Outline 1

Agree

1 **brother played sports, but I didn't**
   - brother = highly competitive
   - me = laid back

2 **sister played sports**
   - hated losing → tried hardest to win
   - is same way today → competitive and tried to be best

Sample Response 1 🎧 Q1_04_4

Agree

Now that I think about it, I believe the statement is correct. When my brother was young, he played on a soccer team. I didn't play sports though. Now that we're older, I have noticed that we have very different personalities. I'm more laid back whereas my brother is highly competitive. I believe the fact that he played soccer made him that way. My sister played sports when she was young as well. She really hated losing, so she always tried her hardest to win. She's the same way today even when she isn't playing sports. She's extremely competitive and tries to be the best no matter what she is doing.

Sample Outline 2

Disagree

1 **never played sports but am competitive**
   - hate losing → do best to win
   - no sports so must get competitiveness from elsewhere

2 **best friend played several sports**
   - excellent athlete but not competitive
   - doesn't care if wins or loses anything

Sample Response 2 Q1_04_5

Disagree

I don't think the statement is correct. Playing sports in your youth doesn't mean that you'll be competitive later in life. I never played sports when I was young, but I'm actually quite competitive. I hate losing, so I do my best to win at everything. Since I didn't play sports, I'm sure that my competitiveness must come from somewhere else. In addition, my best friend at school played several sports in elementary school. He played soccer, baseball, and basketball. He's an excellent athlete, but he's not competitive. In fact, he doesn't seem to care about anything. It doesn't matter to him if he wins or loses whatever he does.

Question 1 #5   p. 26

A

Agree

I strongly agree with the statement. Students like myself are busy all day long, and we sometimes don't have time to eat breakfast or lunch. Because of that, it would be great if we were allowed to eat snacks during class. That would keep us from getting too hungry. In addition, snacks can provide students with energy when they need it. The other day, I was starving in the middle of class. When my teacher wasn't looking, I ate a quick snack. I wasn't supposed to do that. But I felt much better afterward. Since I was able to concentrate in class, I didn't feel bad about eating in class.

Disagree

Students should never be permitted to eat snacks in class. I therefore disagree with the statement. Even if students skip breakfast or lunch, they have time to eat snacks. At my school, there are five minutes between each class. That's plenty of time to eat a small snack. So there's no need to have any snacks during class. Second, if students eat snacks in class, they will cause disruptions. For one thing, the students eating the snacks won't pay attention to the lesson. As a result, they won't learn anything. For another thing, they'll disturb the class by eating, so other students won't be able to pay attention to the teacher.

iBT Practice Test

Sample Outline 1

Doing Exercise Every Day

1 **wanted to lose weight**
   - only exercised when felt like it → didn't lose weight
   - exercised every day → lost lots of weight

2 **can be in good health**
   - parents work out daily
   - got annual checkups → were in perfect health

Sample Response 1 Q1_05_4

Doing Exercise Every Day

Doing exercise every day is a better option than exercising only when you have free time. I used to be overweight, so I decided to lose weight. At first, I only exercised when I felt like it. But I couldn't lose any weight. Finally, I began exercising daily. I immediately lost lots of weight and got in great shape. In addition, by exercising every day, you can make sure that you're in good health. Both of my parents work out at a gym each day. They recently went to the doctor to get their annual checkups. The doctor said they were in perfect health and credited their exercise routines.

Sample Outline 2

Doing Exercise during Free Time

1 **not serious athlete**
   - don't have time to exercise daily
   - only do when have time

2 **dangerous to exercise every day**
   - muscles need rest
   - friend rides bike 20km daily → got bad injury from too much exercise
   - me = exercise 2x/week = never gotten hurt

Doing Exercise during Free Time

Given the two choices, I would prefer to exercise whenever I have free time. First, only serious athletes exercise every day. I'm not a serious athlete. I enjoy exercising, but I don't have time to do it on a daily basis. I therefore only exercise when I have some spare time. Second, it can be dangerous to exercise every day. The body's muscles need rest, and people can suffer injuries if they work out every day. My friend rides her bike twenty kilometers every single day. Recently, she suffered a bad injury from exercising too much. As for me, I exercise around twice a week, and I've never gotten hurt like that before.

Question 1 #6   p. 29

A

Being Very Good at One Activity

There are several advantages to being very good at one activity. For instance, you could probably make money from that activity. My cousin is like that. He's an outstanding baseball player and might become a pro ballplayer one day. Other people can become famous because they can do a single activity very well. There are some disadvantages though. One is that a person might get bored with that activity and not want to do it anymore. Then, that person might not be able to do another activity well. Some people also might only talk about one particular activity with their friends. Their friends might not enjoy hearing about the same topic again and again.

Being Above Average at Several Activities

I can think of a couple of advantages to being above average at several activities. Because a person can do several things well, that person can make many friends. My brother is a member of several clubs, and his friends are all interesting people. A person who's above average at several activities can also do various kinds of work. So that person will always be able to get a job. On the downside, people who are only above average will never become truly great at something. That could destroy the dreams of some people. They will also never become specialists since they focus on many different activities.

iBT Practice Test

Sample Outline 1

Buying Textbooks for Classes

1 advantages
   - underline passages and take notes in books → remember key info
   - keep textbooks forever → have small library of reference materials

2 disadvantages
   - textbooks are expensive → many can't afford
   - math and science = very expensive
   - don't want books when classes end → throw away = waste of money

Sample Response 1 🎧 Q1_06_4

Buying Textbooks for Classes

A big advantage of buying textbooks is that you can underline passages and take notes in them. I do that in my textbooks because that helps me remember key information. I can also keep my textbooks forever. So I have built a small library at home that I can use when I need reference materials. One disadvantage is that some textbooks are expensive. Many people can't afford to buy them. That's especially true about math and science books, which can be extremely expensive. Other people don't want textbooks after their classes end, so they just throw the books away. Buying textbooks is a huge waste of money for them.

Sample Outline 2

Checking Out Books from the Library for Classes

1 advantages
   - costs nothing to borrow from library → save money
   - borrowed books 2 years ago
   - librarian told me about other books → borrowed them → learned more

2 disadvantages
   - some textbooks not at libraries
   - borrow books for limited amount of time
   - went to library to borrow book → was already checked out

Sample Response 2 🎧 Q1_06_5

Checking Out Books from the Library for Classes

The most important advantage is that it costs nothing to borrow books from the library. So students can save money by not purchasing books. I did that two years ago, and it worked out well. In addition, the librarian told me about other books related to my textbooks, so I borrowed them. I therefore learned more thanks to my using the library. However, there are some drawbacks.

Some textbooks aren't available at libraries. And people can only borrow books for a limited amount of time. Once, I went to the library to borrow a textbook. But somebody else had already checked it out, so I couldn't get that book for my class.

Question 1 #7   p. 32

A

I would tell all my friends and family members where I'm going. One reason is that some of my friends and family members might have visited the country before. So they can tell me about good places to go. For instance, my uncle is a world traveler. He has visited dozens of countries and can recommend interesting places to visit. I also don't want to just disappear for a while. It would be rude not to tell people where I'm going. Once, one of my friends traveled abroad for six months but didn't tell anyone. Everyone was worried and thought something bad had happened. I don't want people to worry about me like that.

Tell One or Two Friends or Family Members

I would tell one or two friends or family members where I'm going. For one thing, I'm a private person, so I don't need to tell everyone about my life. I can tell my parents and best friend what I'm doing. Then, they won't worry while I'm gone. For another thing, I don't want people to think I'm bragging about traveling abroad. One of my classmates travels abroad frequently. He's very proud of that and often discusses his trips. Some people think he's showing off because he can afford to travel so much. I don't want people to think badly of me, so I wouldn't discuss traveling unless people asked me about it.

iBT Practice Test

Sample Outline 1

Repairing Roads

1 **use $ for benefit of everyone**
   - all people use roads
   - all residents gain if repair roads

2 **city roads in poor condition**
   - tons of potholes = driving difficult
   - roads not wide enough
   - drivers would be happy if city repaired roads

Sample Response 1   Q1_07_4

Repairing Roads

All three choices would be good uses of the money. But the best usage of it would be to repair the roads in my city. First of all, my city should use the money for the benefit of everyone who lives in it. Everyone uses the roads to go to various places, so all residents would gain from the city repairing the roads. The roads in my city are in poor condition, too. There are tons of potholes, so driving on some roads is difficult. There are also some roads that aren't wide enough. If the city could repair these roads, then drivers in the city would be happy.

Sample Outline 2

Expanding the Local Museum

1 **museum has few exhibits**
   - not many things to see → few people visit
   - if expand museum, more items on display → more people visit

2 **help students learn**
   - local students go to library on field trips
   - if more exhibits, can learn about more topics
   - might become interested in history, archaeology, or biology

Sample Response 2   Q1_07_5

Expanding the Local Museum

I wish the city would use the money to expand the local museum. We have a museum, but it's pretty small. It only has a few exhibits, so there aren't too many things to see. As a result, few people visit the museum nowadays. If the city expanded the museum, it could put more items on display. That would result in more people visiting the museum. A bigger museum would help students learn. Students in my city visit the museum on field trips. If they can see more exhibits, they can learn about more topics. Some might even become interested in fields like history, archaeology, and biology by visiting the museum.

Question 1 #8   p. 35

A

Agree

I strongly agree with the statement. People with a free time should spend some of it doing volunteer work. First, there's a shortage of volunteers everywhere. Many people want to volunteer but are too busy with work and family. So people with free time should help by volunteering. My aunt is a housewife whose children are in college. She has lots of free time, so she volunteers at a homeless shelter. In addition, people with plenty of free time get bored easily. So they can make themselves busy while helping others. They might even learn a new skill if they volunteer at a hospital or similar place.

Disagree

I don't think people with free time need to volunteer, so I disagree with the statement. First, volunteer work should be voluntary. People shouldn't volunteer because others expect them or tell them to do that. Some local schools force students to volunteer. That's not really volunteering, so I think it's wrong for the schools to make students do it. Second, everyone has different ways of spending free time. Some people may want to volunteer whereas others may prefer to play sports or just stay at home and relax. Everyone is different. So it's not right to expect people to volunteer simply because they have some free time.

iBT Practice Test

Sample Outline 1

Shopping at Supermarkets

1 **advantages**
   - wide selection of foods
   - low prices → convenient for shoppers
   - family shops at supermarket → love getting food want + cheap prices

2 **disadvantages**
   - don't sell many foreign foods
   - uncommon foods hard to get
   - mother complains → can't get certain foods she wants

Sample Response 1 ⌒ Q1_08_4

Shopping at Supermarkets

There are plenty of advantages to shopping at supermarkets. For example, supermarkets are big, so they have wide selections of foods. They also usually sell foods at low prices, so that's convenient for shoppers. My family shops at a local supermarket, and we love it. We can get all the food we want for inexpensive prices. One disadvantage is that supermarkets don't sell many foreign foods. Some uncommon foods are also hard to get. My mother sometimes complains that she can't get Indian or Spanish food at our local supermarket. We can't get certain exotic fruits either. Those are the two main disadvantages.

Sample Outline 2

Shopping at Specialty Stores

1 **advantages**
   - outstanding selections of foods
   - deli = numerous cold cuts
   - bakery = wonderful pastry selection
   - quality of food is high → stores focus on one type of item

2 **disadvantages**
   - prices high → best ingredients often imported, so goods cost a lot
   - hard to get to stores
   - parents love cheese store → in another city = takes 1 hour to get there

Sample Response 2 ⌒ Q1_08_5

Shopping at Specialty Stores

The primary advantage of shopping at specialty stores is that they have outstanding selections of foods. For instance, the local deli has numerous cold cuts while the bakery has a wonderful selection of pastries. The quality of the food is high as well because these stores focus on one type of item. On the other hand, the prices at specialty stores tend to be high. They use the best ingredients, which are often imported. So their goods cost a lot. Some specialty stores are hard to get to as well. For instance, there's a cheese mart my parents love. Unfortunately, it's in another city, so it takes more than an hour to go there.

Question 1 #9   p. 38

A

Help Their Employees with Their Personal Development

For me, the choice is obvious. Supervisors should help their employees with their professional development. The major reason is that they can teach their employees how to do their jobs better. Supervisors have lots of experience and know how to work well. They should provide their workers with some of their knowledge. Another reason is that this will help the overall performance of a company. My mother is a supervisor at her company. She always assists her employees with their jobs. As a result, her department's productivity has increased very much. This has enabled her company to do well and to make lots of money.

Let Their Employees Work the Way They Want To

I believe supervisors should let their employees work the way they want to. First, supervisors don't know how to do every job at a company. So they might give bad advice or instructions to some workers. My brother's boss does this. He often tells my brother to do something, but it's bad advice. My brother has to follow the instructions though because he can't ignore his boss. In addition, there are usually multiple ways to do tasks. And everyone is different. It's much better to let workers be creative and do work according to the style that fits them best. Good supervisors realize this and leave their employees alone.

iBT Practice Test

Sample Outline 1

Work Full Time during Summer Vacation

1 **will have plenty of time in summer vacation**
   - can work many hours → save money
   - 2 older bros did that → always had spending money

2 **don't want to work during semester**
   - focus on studies
   - bros' friends worked part time at school → didn't get good grades

Sample Response 1 🎧 Q1_09_4

Work Full Time during Summer Vacation

When I go to university, I intend to work full time during summer vacation to earn spending money. First, I will have plenty of time during summer vacation, so I can work many hours then. That will give me the chance to save money. My two older brothers did that each year in college, and they always had enough spending money. I also don't want to work during the semester. I prefer to focus on my studies instead. My brothers said that some of their friends worked part time at school. But their friends didn't get good grades. I want good grades, so I'll only work during summer.

Sample Outline 2

Take Out a Loan from a Bank

1 **won't have time to work at school**
   - focus on schoolwork
   - sis took out loan → stress level was low since didn't work

2 **student loans = low interest rates**
   - can borrow money but pay back little interest
   - better than using credit card to get cash advances

Sample Response 2 🎧 Q1_09_5

Take Out a Loan from a Bank

I plan to take out a loan from a bank to get spending money. When I attend school, I will need money, but I won't have time to work. I'm going to focus on my

classwork. As a result, taking out a loan is my only option. My sister did that as a university student. She said that her stress level was low since she didn't have to work. That sounds good to me. Another reason is that student loans come with low interest rates. So I can borrow money but won't have to pay back much interest. To me, that's better than using my credit card to take out cash advances.

A

Always Telling the Truth

I can think of some advantages to always telling the truth. One is that people will believe everything you say. My brother is honest even when it could hurt him. People know that, so they believe whatever he says. In addition, people ask honest individuals for advice all the time. They know they will hear the truth even though it might be unwelcome or unpleasant. There are disadvantages though. Sometimes people can get hurt by the truth. My brother sometimes tells people their clothes look bad or their hair is unstylish. That can hurt their feelings. In cases like those, telling white lies would be a bit more convenient.

Being More Polite at Times

One advantage of being more polite at times is that a person can make others feel good. My friend asked me about some cookies she made once. They tasted terrible, but I said they were good. Because I was polite, she was happy. It's also sometimes better to be polite than to be completely honest. There were no advantages to telling my friend the truth about her cookies. Conversely, being polite can harm some people. One time, I told a different friend that he was good at drawing pictures even though he wasn't. He entered an art contest, and people laughed at his pictures. He felt so bad that he never drew pictures again.

iBT Practice Test

Sample Outline 1

Using Public Transportation While on a Trip

1 **advantages**
   - save money → cheaper to take bus or taxi
   - convenient in unfamiliar cities
   - visited Tokyo → got around easily on buses and subways

2 **disadvantages**
- public transportation crowded
- Tokyo subway in rush hour → so many people = couldn't breathe
- wait for bus at bus stop = annoying

Sample Response 1 🎧 Q1_10_4

Using Public Transportation While on a Trip

Using public transportation while on a trip has some benefits. One is that travelers can save money. It's cheaper to take a bus or a taxi than to rent a car. Public transportation is also convenient for people in unfamiliar cities. Last year, my family visited Tokyo. We had never been there before, but we got around easily on buses and subways. As for the drawbacks, public transportation can be crowded. We took the subway in Tokyo during rush hour once, and there were so many people. We felt like we couldn't breathe. We also had to wait for buses sometimes. Waiting at a bus stop was so annoying at times.

Sample Outline 2

Renting a Car While on a Trip

1 **advantages**
- can move around easily
- parents travel on business → always rent vehicles = can go anywhere
- can visit places on own schedules → don't wait for buses or subways

2 **disadvantages**
- can get lost and confused in new city
- dad got lost → 2 hours late for meeting
- rental cars break down or get flat tires
- mother's car towed in other country → unpleasant for her

Sample Response 2 🎧 Q1_10_5

Renting a Car While on a Trip

Renting a car while on a trip has many advantages. Travelers with their own vehicles can move around easily. My parents frequently travel on business, and they always rent vehicles. They like being able to go anywhere. By renting a car, people also can visit places according to their own schedules. They don't have to wait for buses or subways. However, it's easy to get lost and confused in a new city. My dad got lost driving once, so he was two hours late for a meeting. Sometimes rental cars break down or get flat tires, too. My mother's car had to get towed once when she was in another country. That was very unpleasant.

Question 2 #1   p. 51

A

Sample Notes

What Will Happen: students can work part time off campus

Details: - can work for nearby businesses
        - need 3.0 GPA to participate

B

Listening Script

Now listen to two students discussing the announcement.

M Student: This is excellent news. I can't wait to apply for a job in that new program.

W Student: New program?

M: The school is working with local business to provide part-time jobs for students.

W: Interesting. I haven't heard about it.

M: You ought to look into it. It's so hard to get a job on campus nowadays. Most students keep their jobs year after year, so there are rarely openings. I've applied for numerous jobs on campus but have never gotten one.

W: It sounds like you'll be able to get one now.

M: I hope so. Even better, only students with good grades are allowed to take advantage of the program.

W: You qualify, don't you?

M: I sure do. But not everyone who wants a job will qualify. That will work to my advantage since I'll be competing against fewer students. That will give me a great chance to finally get hired.

Sample Notes

Man's Opinion: pleased w/news
First Reason: hard to get job on campus
Details: - few job openings each year
        - applied for jobs → always rejected
Second Reason: only students w/good grades qualify
Details: - reduces number of students competing with
        - increases chances of getting job

C

Sample Response 🎧 Q2_01_2

The students have a conversation about a new work program at the school. According to the announcement, some businesses off campus will hire students part time. Students need a GPA of 3.0 or higher to get a job. The man expresses his support for the new program. He tells the woman that he has applied for many jobs on campus. However, since there are few job openings, he has never been offered a job. Then, he adds that because of the rule about grades, some students aren't eligible for the program. He believes this fact will increase his chances of getting a job since fewer students will apply for positions. The man thus thinks he will be able to get hired this semester.

iBT Practice Test

Sample Notes - READING

Engineering library = getting enlarged

- will be closed June 1 – August 24
- no books and journals available then

Listening Script

Now listen to two students discussing the notice.

W Student: Did you hear the news? Fulton Library is getting expanded.

M Student: That's cool. Uh, wait a minute . . . When is this happening?

W: This summer. When we return to school, it's going to be much bigger. Isn't that great?

M: Um . . . Not really. I was planning to spend most of my summer studying there.

W: Why don't you just study at the main library?

M: Well, as an engineer, I prefer studying there. I feel uncomfortable when I have to study at the main library.

W: I guess you've got to do that this summer though. And you won't have access to any books there.

M: Seriously? Oh, no. This is awful. I was planning on doing an independent study course with Professor Cormack this summer. I might have to cancel that now.

W: You'd better talk to him at once.

M: You're right. I need to find him immediately to

discuss how the library work is going to affect my studies.

Man → dislikes announcement

1 **wants to study at library in summer**
   - is engineer → feels comfortable there
   - feels uncomfortable at main library

2 **wants to take independent study class in summer**
   - no access to books this summer
   - may need to cancel class

Sample Response 🎧 Q2_01_4

During their conversation, the man and woman talk about the notice by the university library. It reads that the school's engineering library is going to be closed for the summer. The reason is that it will be expanded during that time to let it hold more books and students. The man dislikes this announcement for two reasons. The first is that he wants to study at the engineering library this summer. He doesn't want to have to visit the school's main library. The second reason he mentions is that he wants to do an independent study project this summer. Because no books will be available during the summer, he is worried that he might be unable to do the project.

Question 2 #2   p. 54

A

Sample Notes

The Letter Writer's Opinion: students should not have double majors

Details: - grades go down when have 2 majors
         - should have 1 major → can focus on it

B

Listening Script

Now listen to two students discussing the letter.

W Student: I'm going to try for a double major in History and Archaeology.

M Student: You won't be able to do that if a professor in the Sociology Department gets her way.

W: I read that letter in the newspaper. It was so silly.

M: I agree, but I'm curious why you think that way.

W: First of all, everyone has different abilities. Some students can't handle the extra workload, but others can. We shouldn't punish good students merely because poor students can't do something.

M: That makes a lot of sense.

W: And there's another thing . . .

M: What?

W: Well, grades aren't really that important. What's crucial is the knowledge we learn in our classes. So, um, it's much better for me to acquire knowledge in two fields than just one. The professor seems to be against people becoming as educated as possible. If you ask me, that's a terrible attitude to have.

Sample Notes

Woman's Opinion: disagrees w/letter
First Reason: some students can handle workload
Details: - students have different abilities
         - shouldn't punish good students for something bad students can't do
Second Reason: knowledge learned > grades
Details: - better to get knowledge in 2 fields than 1
         - thinks professor is against education

C

Sample Response 🎧 Q2_02_2

During the conversation, the woman explains why she disagrees with the letter to the editor. The letter was written by a professor in the Sociology Department. The professor argues that students should not be permitted to have double majors. Instead, they should only have one major so that they can keep their grades up. The woman's first statement in opposition to this belief is that not all students are the same. The woman says there are good and bad students. She believes good students can successfully get double majors, so they shouldn't be penalized because bad students cannot do that. Secondly, the woman feels that knowledge is more important than grades. Thus, students with double majors can get more knowledge no matter what their grades are.

iBT Practice Test

Sample Notes — READING

New procedure for waiting list

- students late to class get put on it
- if on waiting list after 2 weeks, can't enroll

Listening Script

Now listen to two students discussing the announcement.

W Student: I can't believe it. This new policy regarding the waiting list is awful.

M Student: Why do you say that? I kind of like it.

W: Way too many things could go wrong.

M: Such as what?

W: I've got one class in Brandon Hall and another right after it in Claremont Hall. They're across campus from each other. If my first class finishes late, I won't get to my second class in time. What if I get put on the waiting list in that class? It's not fair.

M: Hmm . . . You'd better run to class in that case.

W: I guess so. Plus, uh, seniors and juniors always register first because they need to enroll in some classes to graduate. But if they get placed on a waiting list and then can't take a class, that could prevent them from graduating. That would be a horrible outcome.

M: Oh, yeah. I don't think the school considered that.

Sample Notes — LISTENING

Woman → objects to policy

1 **classes far from each other**
  - class finishes late → will be late for next class
  - if gets put on waiting list, not fair

2 **juniors and seniors register first**
  - need to take classes to graduate
  - if get put on waiting list, might not graduate

Sample Response 🎧 Q2_02_4

The two speakers discuss the policy change explained in the announcement. From now on, when too many students sign up for a class, the waiting list will be determined in a new way. Professors will observe which students are late for class, and then those students will get put on the waiting list. The woman strongly objects to this policy. She mentions that she has back-to-back classes in buildings on opposite sides of the campus. If the first class gets out late, she could be late for her next class and thereby be placed on the waiting list. She then complains that juniors and seniors who are late could be put on the waiting list, too. Then, if they aren't allowed in the class, they might not be able to graduate.

Question 2 #3 p. 57

A

Sample Notes

What Will Happen: new webpage for musicians and singers

Details: - can communicate and exchange info
       - form groups and schedule concerts

B

Listening Script

Now listen to two students discussing the announcement.

M Student: I'm really pleased we're going to have a new website for musicians.

W Student: What's so special about it? Aren't there plenty of those for people in the local area?

M: There are, but this one is specifically for students here.

W: Um, okay. I don't get it though.

M: It's simple. My rock band needs a drummer. We've been advertising on some websites, but the only people who have answered live too far away to meet regularly.

W: Oh, I see.

M: So if we can find a drummer on campus, it'll be easier to get together for rehearsals and concerts. Plus, if the drummer is someone in our age group, we'll be able to relate to one another better.

W: Right.

M: And speaking of concerts, we can schedule them more easily now. We haven't had many concerts because it's hard to find places to play at. But this website should solve that problem.

Sample Notes

Man's Opinion: in favor of website
First Reason: band needs drummer
Details: - find one on campus = can meet for rehearsals and concerts
       - if drummer is same age, can relate better
Second Reason: easy to schedule concerts
Details: - had few concerts → hard to find places to play at
       - website should change that

C

Sample Response 🎧 Q2_03_2

In their conversation, the man and woman discuss the new website described in the announcement. The Music

Department is making a website for student musicians and singers. They'll be able to get in touch with other people who like music. Then, they can form bands and arrange concerts more easily. The man speaks favorably about the website for a couple of reasons. The first is that his own band needs a drummer. They've advertised on other websites but haven't found anyone that can join their band yet. However, by advertising on the school's website, they should be able to find a drummer close to their ages. Next, he remarks that his band hasn't played many concerts because they're hard to schedule. He believes the new website will help his band arrange some performances.

iBT Practice Test

Sample Notes — READING

Theater and performing arts club to form

- will put on a play each semester
- meetings will be rehearsals + lessons to improve acting skills

Listening Script

Now listen to two students discussing the notice.

M Student: Stacy, did you see that a club focusing on the theater is forming this semester?

W Student: I did, so I'll definitely be attending the meeting this Saturday.

M: That's good news for you.

W: You can say that again. I missed the audition for the play the Drama Department is sponsoring this semester. I'm, uh, I'm looking forward to being able to perform in the play this club is going to put on.

M: That should get you the acting experience you want.

W: Exactly. There's another advantage as well.

M: There is? What is it?

W: The club is also going to have lessons on improving acting techniques. As you know, I'm not an experienced actress. I love performing, but I need to get better at certain aspects of it. If the club members get some lessons, I should be able to improve significantly.

M: Good luck.

Sample Notes — LISTENING

Woman → pleased about new club

1 **wants to perform in play**
   - missed audition for Drama Department play
   - wants to get acting experience

2 **lessons on improving acting techniques**
   - not experienced → needs to get better
   - lessons should help improve

Sample Response 🎧 Q2_03_4

The conversation is about a new club that is being formed. According to the notice, a drama club is being established. The members of the club will put on a play each semester. When they meet, they'll both rehearse for the play and get some acting lessons. The woman is pleased to hear the news about the club, so she's going to join it. She mentions that she couldn't act in the Drama Department's play. She's very happy that she'll get the chance to perform in the club's play. She hopes to gain experience by doing that. The woman is also looking forward to getting some acting lessons. She needs to become a better actress, so she hopes she can improve her technique thanks to the lessons.

Question 2 #4   p. 60

A

Sample Notes

The Letter Writer's Opinion: dormitories shockingly bad
Details: - old facilities with problems and small rooms
        - school should renovate dorms to improve them

B

Listening Script

Now listen to two students discussing the letter.

W Student: That guy who complained about the dorms in the paper must have pretty high standards.

M Student: What makes you say that? A great deal of what he wrote is correct.

W: I disagree. He complained about the facilities in the dorms, but the ones in mine are fine. After all, uh, there's plenty of hot water in the showers, and the lights are fine.

M: What about the Internet connection? Mine is slow.

W: Not mine. There are no Wi-Fi problems in Kimberly Hall.

M: Okay, but you have to admit that the dorms should be renovated.

W: Where's the money going to come from? That's the biggest issue in my mind.

M: How so?

W: Tuition is already extremely high. Renovating the dorms will cost millions of dollars. That will lead the school to raise tuition even more. I'd rather pay less money and have the conditions of the dorms remain the same.

Woman's Opinion: disagrees w/letter

First Reason: dorm facilities are fine

Details: - lots of hot water and good lights
- no Wi-Fi problems

Second Reason: should not renovate dorms

Details: - will cost a lot → tuition = too high
- would raise tuition even more

C

Q2_04_2

The woman expresses her disagreement with the letter writer in her conversation with the man. The letter writer dislikes the dorms on campus. He points out that the facilities are bad, the rooms are small, and the buildings need repairing. The woman tells the man two problems she has with the letter writer. The first is that she disagrees with his opinion about the dorms themselves. She states that the hot water and lights in her dorm are fine. She also remarks that the Wi-Fi works well in her dormitory. The second point she brings up is that renovating the dorms will be expensive. If the school does that, it will raise tuition. The woman states that tuition is already too high, so she prefers that no renovations be done.

iBT Practice Test

New apartment complex open

- has many types of apartments and facilities
- students can get 10% discount on rent

Now listen to two students discussing the advertisement.

W Student: Jason, are you still looking for a place to live next semester?

M Student: Yeah. I haven't had any luck so far though.

W: What about Bayside Gardens?

M: I'd love to live there, but it hasn't opened yet. It's still under construction.

W: Not according to this ad. Apparently, you can rent apartments there now.

M: Seriously? That's awesome.

W: Uh, out of curiosity, what's so great about it?

M: You can't beat the location. The places I've looked at are thirty minutes away from school. But Bayside

Gardens is much closer. Talk about convenient.

W: Yeah, I think it's like two or three minutes away from here.

M: Plus, I heard students can get a cheaper rate. That means I can pay less to stay there than I would at all the other apartment buildings nearby.

W: You'd better check it out fast then. I bet other students are interested in it, too.

Man → interested in the ad

1 **likes the location**
- other places are 30 minutes from school
- Bayside Gardens is closer

2 **students can get cheaper rate**
- can pay less money
- cheaper than other apartment buildings

Q2_04_4

During their conversation, the woman talks about an advertisement for an apartment complex. According to the ad, the complex is brand new and close to campus. There are many types of units available for students. Students can also pay lower rent if they show their ID cards. The man is extremely interested in the advertisement since he is currently looking for a place to stay. When the woman asks him about the complex, he mentions the location first. He comments that it's a lot closer to school than any other apartment complexes. He finds that very convenient. After that, he brings up the fact that the rent at the complex is cheaper than at other apartments. If he gets an apartment there, he can save money.

Question 2 #5 p. 63

A

What Will Happen: students can't work 20+hours/week on campus

Details: - depriving others of jobs
- must have hours reduced

B

Now listen to two students discussing the announcement.

W Student: I'm so frustrated by the school's decision to reduce the number of hours we can work.

M Student: How many hours do you work?

W: Thirty-five hours a week at two jobs.

M: Really? Why do you work so much?

W: I need to earn enough money for tuition. If I don't work, I can't afford to study here. Because of this new rule, I'll have to quit one of my jobs.

M: I'm sorry to hear that. But, uh, do you think you could find another job? Uh, like one off campus?

W: I'm going to have to do that.

M: So this new regulation won't hurt you too much.

W: On the contrary, it will. I'll have to travel off campus, so I'll lose time and money. And it will be harder to arrange my schedule at a place off campus. My employer won't care about my classes like my employers here do.

Sample Notes

Woman's Opinion: opposed to decision
First Reason: needs to work to pay tuition
Details: - can't afford school if doesn't work
　　　　 - but will have to quit one job
Second Reason: has to get job off campus
Details: - will lose time and money
　　　　 - will be harder to arrange schedule

C

Sample Response ◠ Q2_05_2

The students discuss the announcement by the school administration. A new rule is being implemented. Students with on-campus jobs are no longer permitted to work more than twenty hours a week. The woman is strongly opposed to this decision by the school. She has two jobs and works thirty-five hours each week. She states that she needs to earn money to pay tuition. But she's going to have to quit one of her jobs. In response to the man's suggestion that she work off campus, she answers that she will do that. However, she says she'll have to travel to the job, which will take time and cost money. And it will be hard to make a work schedule because of her classes. So she's going to be hurt by the decision.

iBT Practice Test

Sample Notes — READING

Vending machines in buildings to be removed

- sell junk food → affecting health of students
- students should eat healthy foods

Listening Script

Now listen to two students discussing the announcement.

M Student: Hold on, Deanna. I want to get a snack before class starts . . . Uh, wait a minute. Where did the vending machine go?

W Student: Haven't you heard? The dean had them removed.

M: Huh? What did he do that for?

W: He made an announcement in which he wrote that students weren't eating properly.

M: It's none of his business what I eat. Plus, it's not like I'm eating candy bars for lunch and dinner. I just want a snack to eat in between classes.

W: The dean suggested eating healthier foods. I happen to agree with him.

M: Hmm . . . I don't see any cafés here in Robinson Hall. So how are we supposed to eat healthy food if none is available?

W: We could go to the student center.

M: Er . . . That's a fifteen-minute walk from here. We only have ten minutes in between classes. It's literally impossible to get healthy food for a snack in between classes.

Sample Notes — LISTENING

Man → against decision

1 **none of dean's business what he eats**
   - isn't eating bad food for meals
   - just wants a snack

2 **no place to eat healthy food in building**
   - could go to student center → 15 minutes away
   - no time to go there in between classes

Sample Response ◠ Q2_05_4

During their conversation, the man learns about the announcement made by the dean of engineering. The dean had the vending machines removed from a couple of buildings. He doesn't want the students to eat junk food. Instead, he tells the students to eat healthy food. The man is strongly against the dean's decision. The first point he brings up is that his diet is none of the dean's business. He also states that he only wants a candy bar for a snack, not a meal. The second point he mentions is that there's nowhere in the building to buy healthy snacks. He remarks that the student center is far away from the building. He therefore can't go there, get a snack, and return in between his classes.

A

Sample Notes

What Will Happen: campus bicycle lanes to be removed

Details: - lanes used by few cyclists

         - cyclists must ride on roads

B

Listening Script

Now listen to two students discussing the notice.

W Student: Josh, you cycle a lot, don't you? What are your thoughts on the decision by the school to remove the bicycle lanes?

M Student: I think it's a very poor decision.

W: Can you elaborate a bit?

M: First of all, now cyclists have to ride on the streets. That's going to be dangerous for everyone on a bike. You know, uh, I bet there will be more accidents involving cyclists and motor vehicles because of this.

W: You may be right about that. I hope you don't get hurt.

M: Thanks for saying that. Oh, another problem is that it's going to take longer to get to classes now.

W: Huh? What do you mean?

M: By using the bike lanes, I could arrive at my classes fast since there was little traffic on them. But now that I have to cycle with cars on the road, it will take longer to get to classes. I'll have to leave earlier for class now.

Sample Notes

Man's Opinion: thinks is poor decision

First Reason: cyclists on streets = dangerous

Details: - thinks will be more accidents w/cyclists and
           motor vehicles

Second Reason: will take longer to get to classes

Details: - when used bike lanes, could travel fast

        - if cycle on road, will take longer

        - will have to leave earlier for class

C

Sample Response   Q2_06_2

The man and the woman discuss a recent decision by the Buildings and Grounds Department to get rid of the bicycle lanes on campus. The notice points out that few people use the lanes, so they aren't needed. Cyclists have to ride on the streets from now on. The man is opposed to this decision for a couple of reasons. The

first is that he thinks cyclists will be in danger without the lanes. Cyclists have to use the streets, so he believes cars are going to hit cyclists more often. He also complains that it will take him a long time to get to his classes. The reason is that he will have to ride in traffic instead of in the bicycle lanes.

iBT Practice Test

Sample Notes READING

all students must take Western civ classes

- year-long course
- must get letter grade
- no exemptions for any students

Listening Script

Now listen to two students discussing the announcement.

M Student: Oh, no! I totally forgot about the requirement to take the Western civilization classes.

W Student: What? How could you forget? It's all that everyone on campus has been talking about these days.

M: Well, uh, I guess I just don't want to take the classes.

W: Not me. I'm looking forward to them. I think it's important to learn about the great accomplishments from the past. I want to find out more about who helped create the society we live in today.

M: Yeah, I understand that, but I have other classes I want to take.

W: So do I, so I completely understand the problem about having two more required classes to take. But I don't think it's a problem that you can't solve.

M: Oh, yeah? So what are you going to do?

W: I'm going to take Western Civilization 101 this semester and 102 in the spring semester. Then, I'll stay on campus for summer school and enroll in a couple of other required classes then. As I see it, it's not a particularly big problem to solve.

Sample Notes LISTENING

Woman → supports new requirement

1 **looking forward to taking classes**
   - important to learn about past accomplishments
   - find out more about people who created society

2 **no problem to take extra required classes**
   - will take one class this semester + next class in spring
   - will take summer school → do required classes then

The speakers talk to each other about an announcement by the dean of students. It reminds the students that all of them must take two classes in Western civilization in order to graduate. The woman supports this new requirement by the school. She tells the man the two reasons why she is in favor of it. The first reason is that she wants to know more about the past. She says that she would like to know about the people who helped create modern society. The second reason is that she doesn't consider taking two more requirements a problem. She is planning to enroll in the classes during the fall and spring semesters. Then, she will take other required classes she needs in order to graduate during summer school.

Question 2 #7   p. 69

A

Sample Notes

What Will Happen: student clubs must pay fee to use classroom

Details: - $50 for two hours
          - $20 for each additional hour
          - must rent room for at least two hours

B

Listening Script

Now listen to two students discussing the announcement.

M Student: Take a look at this. I guess we need to pay some money before our photography club meeting this Friday.

W Student: Yeah, I saw that this morning. You know, I don't like this decision, but I understand it.

M: What do you mean?

W: Well, the clubs are using the rooms, and that costs electricity. Many students make messes in the rooms, too. If they don't clean up after themselves, the janitors have extra work to do. So I understand why we have to pay.

M: Yeah, that makes sense.

W: On the other hand . . .

M: Yes?

W: Fifty dollars is a lot of money. And students have to pay that money. That can be expensive for some people, especially if there aren't many people in a club. For big clubs, members can each pay a dollar or two. For small ones, room rentals could get

expensive. So those clubs might not be able to meet too often, and that's not good for them.

Sample Notes

Woman's Opinion: mixed feelings about announcement
First Reason: clubs should pay to use rooms
Details: - use electricity
          - students make messes but don't clean → janitors have extra work
Second Reason: $50 is lot of money
Details: - expensive for some students if small club
          - small clubs might not meet too often

C

Sample Response 🎧 Q2_07_2

The two students are having a discussion about an announcement by the student activities office. According to it, student clubs can have meetings in empty classrooms. However, they need to pay money to rent the room. The fee is a minimum of $50. The woman has mixed feelings about the announcement. First, she understands the reason for the fee. The clubs will use electricity when they're meeting in a room, and the rooms need to be cleaned after they are used, too. However, she thinks the cost is too high. She says that some small clubs will have problems paying the money. Because of that, those clubs might not meet very often. She does not believe that is something positive for the students.

iBT Practice Test

Sample Notes ── READING

Students in dorm must pay security deposit

- costs $250
- rooms checked for damage
- no damage = get money back
- damage = cost of repairing damage removed from deposit

Listening Script

Now listen to two students discussing the notice.

W Student: What? Where am I going to get another $250? This is outrageous!

M Student: You're referring to the deposits we have to pay on our dorm rooms, aren't you?

W: Yes, I am. I'm furious, and you should be, too.

M: On the contrary, I have no problems with the deposit.

W: What? Why not?

M: Too many students are damaging their rooms

nowadays. They're breaking the furniture or causing problems to the walls. They should be responsible for paying for the damage.

W: But I can't come up with that much money.

M: I totally sympathize with your situation. However, if the students don't pay for repairs, then the school has to. And that money will come out of the school's general fund. It normally goes to students. So if it's used to repair rooms, the entire student body will suffer. I actually wish the school had required these deposits earlier than now.

Sample Notes LISTENING

Man → no problems w/deposit

1 **too many students damaging rooms**
   - breaking furniture + causing problems to walls
   - students should pay for damage

2 **if students don't pay, school must**
   - money comes from school's general fund → usually goes to students
   - if use that money, entire student body suffers

Sample Response 🎧 Q2_07_4

The students are having a talk about an announcement by the student housing office. From now on, students living in the dormitories on campus have to pay a $250 security deposit. The money will be returned to the students if their dorm rooms are fine when they leave. But money will be taken from the deposit if their rooms are damaged. The man agrees with this decision. He tells the woman that too many students are damaging their rooms and breaking the furniture. He thinks students should pay for the damage. He also says that if students don't pay, then the money for repairs will come out of the school's general fund. That will negatively affect all of the students, so he supports the security deposits.

Question 2 #8   p. 72

A

Sample Notes

What Will Happen: squash courts available at gym
Details: - first-come, first-served basis
        - can rent racquets → $4/hour

B

Listening Script

Now listen to two students discussing the notice.

M Student: Suzie, we have some time before our next class. Let's go to the gym and play squash for the next half hour.

W Student: No problem, Jeff. But I don't have any money on me.

M: Why do you need money?

W: It costs money to rent racquets. The price is four dollars an hour per racquet, so we need eight dollars.

M: You know, this is the kind of thing I really dislike. Tuition is already sky high, but the school is still coming up with ways to make more money from us. It's ridiculous to have to pay to rent racquets.

W: Yeah, I know what you're saying.

M: And it's not right for us to be charged for an entire hour either. We only have time to play for thirty minutes. We should only be charged for half an hour.

W: Why don't we hang out at the student center instead? We can do something there.

M: Good thinking. Let's go.

Sample Notes

Man's Opinion: unhappy about announcement
First Reason: thinks school is trying to make money from students
Details: - says tuition is sky high
        - ridiculous to pay to rent racquets
Second Reason: shouldn't be charged for entire hour
Details: - only have 30 minutes
        - should be charged for half an hour

C

Sample Response 🎧 Q2_08_2

During their conversation, the students talk about the gym's policy for its squash courts. Students have to pay $4 an hour to rent a racquet to play squash. The man is unhappy about this policy. He tells the woman two reasons why he is opposed to it. The first is that he dislikes that the school is trying to make money by renting racquets. He mentions that tuition at the school is very high, but the school is still trying to get more money from the students. He believes that's wrong. He also doesn't want to be charged for an entire hour. He and the woman only have time to play for half an hour. He thinks they should have to pay half price instead of full price.

iBT Practice Test

Sample Notes — READING

Can sign up for mentoring program

- meet mentee 2x/week
- help w/homework, play games, or be good friend
- no $ but get course credit

Listening Script

Now listen to two students discussing the announcement.

W Student: Mark, do you want to be a mentor? I'm going to register for the new program today.

M Student: Sorry, Christine, but I'm not good with kids.

W: That's too bad. Many of the children in this neighborhood come from broken families, so they only live with one parent. That parent is typically too busy working to take good care of the kid.

M: Uh, huh.

W: So maybe I can help out. You know, I could help a young girl improve her situation. Maybe I could assist her with her homework or something.

M: What do you get out of it?

W: I will get the satisfaction of helping someone in need. Plus, I will get course credit, so that's nice. I need another elective, and volunteering will count. I already asked my advisor.

M: You know, uh, you've convinced me. Let's do it together.

W: I knew I could get you to do it. Let's see if we can mentor kids from the same school.

Sample Notes — LISTENING

Woman → supports program

1 **many children come from broken families**
- live w/one parent → too busy working to take care of kid
- wants to help young girl improve situation

2 **will benefit from program**
- gets satisfaction from helping someone
- gets course credit → will count as elective

Sample Response 🎧 Q2_08_4

The speakers have a discussion about a new program by the Child Studies Department. It is offering students the chance to mentor local children. Mentors won't make any money, but they'll get course credit. They'll also be able to affect the lives of the children they help in a good way. The woman supports the new program and is planning to become a mentor. In trying to convince the man to be a mentor, she gives two reasons for supporting the program. First, she says that many local children only live

with one parent. She thinks she can be a good influence on a child as a mentor. She also says that she will get credit for an elective, and she is happy about that.

Question 2 #9   p. 75

A

Sample Notes

What Will Happen: wages of student workers to rise

Details: - increase by $2/hour
- provide financial assistance to students
- maybe some students work fewer hours → spend more time on studies

B

Listening Script

Now listen to two students discussing the announcement.

M Student: I'm really pleased that student workers will get pay raises next semester. That will mean a few extra dollars a week.

W Student: I work ten hours a week at the library. So I guess I'll make twenty dollars more per week.

M: You must be happy.

W: Hmm . . . Yes and no. I'm definitely glad to be making extra money. Now, um, I'll be able to order pizza or Chinese takeout every once in a while.

M: But it appears you think there's a downside to this move. What could possibly be wrong with making more money?

W: Well, the announcement points out that the school hopes students can work fewer hours since they'll be making more money, right?

M: Yes. So . . . ?

W: As for me, I want to work more hours now to make even more money. So I might have less time to study. In a way, it's likely that this decision will backfire on the university.

Sample Notes

Woman's Opinion: has mixed feelings

First Reason: glad to make extra money

Details: - can order food sometimes

Second Reason: school hopes students work fewer hours

Details: - woman wants to work more hours → make more money
- may have less time to study
- decision may backfire on university

C

The topic of the speakers' discussion is a decision by the student employment office. Beginning in the new year, all student workers will be paid an extra $2 for each hour they work. The school hopes that the extra money will let students work fewer hours. Then, they can focus more on their schoolwork. The woman has mixed feelings about the announcement. She says that she's happy to make more money. She mentions that she will be able to order food more often with the extra money. But she comments that there might be an unexpected result. She states that she wants to work more hours in order to make more money. So she believes the school's decision might not work as planned.

iBT Practice Test

Sample Notes READING

Library will get rid of 5,000 books

- books haven't been checked out for 10+ years
- being removed to increase shelf space
- removed books will be available for purchase

Listening Script

Now listen to two students discussing the announcement.

M Student: What a shortsighted decision. Libraries should be keeping books, not throwing them away.

W Student: But, uh, what about the reason the announcement mentions? You know, the library needs more space.

M: It was renovated two years ago. The amount of shelf space increased more than fifty percent, so I don't believe this excuse. There are plenty of empty shelves throughout the library.

W: I wasn't aware of that. I mostly go there to study, not to borrow books.

M: There's another thing the library hasn't considered.

W: What's that?

M: Simply because people are not checking out books doesn't mean they aren't being used.

W: Um . . . I'm not sure what you mean.

M: I frequently take books off the shelves because I want to read a page or two. I don't borrow them. I merely copy some pages. So the books are useful even though they don't get checked out. Maybe some books the library is throwing out are ones like those.

Sample Notes LISTENING

Man → shortsighted decision by library

1 **library has plenty of shelf space**
   - renovated 2 years ago → increased shelf space by 50%
   - many empty shelves in library

2 **people use books but don't check them out**
   - may take book off shelves and copy pages from it
   - but doesn't borrow → book is still useful
   - library may throw out some useful books

Sample Response Q2_09_4

The university library has announced that it will be disposing of around 5,000 books in summer. The speakers talk about this decision. The university notes that the books it's getting rid of haven't been checked out in more than ten years. It needs to remove the books to get more shelf space. The man tells the woman two reasons why he disagrees with this decision. The first reason is that the library doesn't need more shelf space. It was renovated two years ago, and there are many empty shelves in the library now. The second reason is that he often copies pages from books but doesn't check them out. He thinks some of the books he uses like that may get thrown away.

Question 2 #10   p. 78

A

Sample Notes

What Will Happen: faculty parking lot being expanded

Details: - must drop by September 15
   - has space for 150 vehicles now → will increase to 220 vehicles
   - will let faculty members park near classrooms
   - will remove picnic area to expand parking lot

B

Listening Script

Now listen to two students discussing the notice.

W Student: I'm really looking forward to this weekend's picnic with the members of the French club.

M Student: So am I, uh, especially since we won't be able to have picnics there anymore once the new year starts.

W: Oh, yeah, uh, I had forgotten about that. I can't believe the school is doing that.

M: I know, but professors need a place to park.

W: I live in Walker Hall, so I see that parking lot every day. There are always empty spaces. The school doesn't need to expand the parking lot. When the new lot is finished, it will probably be half empty most of the time.

M: Huh. I wasn't aware of that.

W: In addition, the picnic area is one of the most popular places on campus. Students are always hanging out there. But now the school is taking away one of the best spots on campus. It's not fair.

M: Maybe we should complain to the administration. That might help.

Sample Notes

Woman's Opinion: unhappy about expansion

First Reason: sees parking lot every day → many empty spaces

Details: - school doesn't need to expand lot
- when finish lot, will be half empty most of time

Second Reason: picnic area is popular place on campus

Details: - many students hang out there
- school taking away one of best spots → not fair

C

Sample Response Q2_10_2

The students are having a talk about the decision by the university administration to expand the size of the faculty parking lot. When the parking lot is finished, there will be many more spaces for professors' vehicles. The picnic area will be used to make the lot bigger. The woman is opposed to this decision by the school. She mentions that she sees the parking lot every day. According to her, there are already empty parking spots. She thinks that the lot doesn't need to be expanded. She also remarks that the picnic area is very popular with students on campus. She thinks that it isn't fair for the school to be getting rid of a place that students like to use so much.

iBT Practice Test

Sample Notes READING

Not enough places to study in library

- should keep classrooms open until 2 A.M.
- give students private places to study
- will let students learn more

Listening Script

Now listen to two students discussing the letter.

M Student: Isabelle, you've often complained about not being able to find a seat in the library. What do you think of this proposal?

W Student: That's a good question. I see advantages and disadvantages.

M: What's one benefit?

W: That's obvious. Students can study in places other than the library or their dorm rooms. I hate studying in my dorm because it's so noisy. So I would love to have my own classroom to study in until late at night.

M: Yeah, that makes a lot of sense.

W: But one disadvantage is that the school can't have students studying in hundreds of classrooms across campus every night.

M: How come?

W: Somebody is going to have to lock all those rooms at two in the morning. Who's going to do that? The custodians don't work that late at night. So the school will have to hire a lot more employees to go around just to lock up the rooms.

Sample Notes LISTENING

Woman → has mixed feelings about letter

1 **can give students places to study**
- can't study in dorm since is too noisy
- would love to have classroom to study in

2 **school can't let students study in 100s of classrooms**
- somebody needs to lock up rooms → who will do?
- school will need to hire many people to lock up rooms

Sample Response Q2_10_4

The students talk about a letter to the editor in the school newspaper. The writer of the letter complains that there aren't enough seats for students to study in the library. He would like for the school to allow students to study in empty classrooms until two in the morning. The woman has mixed feelings about the letter writer's suggestion. She thinks it would be beneficial because it would give students quiet places to study. She mentions that she hates studying in her dormitory because it's loud, so she would like to be able to study in a classroom. She also mentions a disadvantage. She points out that the school would need to hire more workers to lock up all of the classrooms late at night.

A

Sample Notes

Main Idea of the Passage: organisms adapt over time

Details: - usually takes multiple generations

- evolution in action = fast evolution

B

Listening Script

Now listen to a lecture on this topic in a biology class.

W Professor: We normally think of evolution as something happening over a period of thousands or even millions of years. That's not always the case though. In some instances, adaptations happen so fast that we can see significant changes from one generation to the next.

For example . . . Think of the cane toad in Australia. This invasive species migrates toward food sources like, uh, like an army advancing in war. Interestingly, scientists have discovered that the cane toads at the front of the invasion are different. They have longer, stronger legs than the toads in the back. This adaptation lets them move faster over longer distances. Thus, they can reach food sources before other toads that haven't evolved.

Another example is the peppered moth in Britain. Before the Industrial Revolution, it was mostly whitish in color. Only about, um, two percent were dark colored. But the environment soon became covered in soot from factories. The white moths stood out, so predators easily saw them. Dark-colored moths could hide better in the soot. More dark-colored moths survived, and, by the end of the 1800s, ninety-eight percent of all peppered moths were dark in color.

Sample Notes

Thesis Statement: sometimes adaptations happen fast
First Example: Australian cane toad
Details: - migrates toward food → toads in front evolve
    - have longer, stronger legs → move faster over longer distances
Second Example: peppered moth → was mostly whitish
Details: - during Industrial Revolution, lots of soot
    - predators found white moths
    - dark-colored moths hid better → became 98% of all peppered moths

C

Sample Response Q3_01_2

The professor talks to the students about changes in two different animals. First, she mentions the cane toad. She says the toads move together as they go to food sources. But she points out that the toads at the front have evolved to have longer and stronger legs than the toads at the back. Next, she mentions the peppered moth. According to her, almost all peppered moths in Britain were white. Then, during the Industrial Revolution, there was a lot of soot, so the white moths were easily spotted by predators. As a result, the moths changed so that nearly all of them were dark colored. Both animals are examples of evolution in action. This is when evolution happens from generation to generation instead of over a long period of time.

iBT Practice Test

Sample Notes READING

Alarm calls → warn other animals of predators

- false alarm calls → no predators but animals flee
- animal making call alone → can eat other animals' food

Listening Script

Now listen to a lecture on this topic in a biology class.

W Professor: This animal you're looking at is the African fork-tailed drongo. That's spelled D-R-O-N-G-O. This small bird practices something called kleptoparasitism. In other words, it steals food from other animals. It doesn't just steal from members of its own species but also takes food from other birds and even mammals.

The fork-tailed drongo eats insects and small reptiles. It hunts on its own and gets food through the efforts of other animals. Here's what it does . . . The drongo follows another animal and watches it gather food. Then, the drongo startles the animal with a call indicating that a predator is near. If the animal gets frightened off, the drongo grabs the food and eats it. Interestingly, the drongo can mimic the sounds of other birds as well as mammals, such as the meerkat.

According to a recent study, the drongo's trick doesn't always work. Some animals don't run away if the warning call is too short. Others wait to see if a predator is actually close at hand. When they see none, they don't flee. As a result, the drongo's trick only accounts for about a quarter of its daily food supply.

African fork-tailed drongo

1 **steals food from animals**
   - watches animal gather food → makes false alarm call
   - animal gets frightened → drongo takes food

2 **doesn't always work**
   - some animals don't run
   - others wait to see if predator is there

Sample Response 🎧 Q3_01_4

In her lecture, the professor discusses a habit of the African fork-tailed drongo. According to her, the drongo gets about a quarter of its food supply from other animals. Basically, it steals food from other animals. The drongo watches animals find food, and then it makes a call. The call it makes is a false animal alarm call. This is a sound which some animals make that warns other animals about nearby predators even though no predators are actually in the area. If an animal believes there is a predator around, it will drop the food and flee. In that case, the false animal alarm call works because the drongo is all alone. It can then take the animal's food and eat it for itself.

Question 3 #2   p. 84

A

Sample Notes

Main Idea of the Passage: the you-too fallacy → respond to accuser by saying, "You, too"

Details: - asserts is doing nothing wrong
        - logical fallacy → other's behavior doesn't excuse actions of first person

B

Listening Script

Now listen to a lecture on this topic in a psychology class.

M Professor: Have you ever been criticized by someone? I'm sure all of you have received criticism at some point in your lives. When you hear a negative comment, you probably want to, uh, turn the tables on the individual making the comment. That's especially true if the person making the criticism is guilty of the same behavior.

Here's an example of what I mean . . . My older brother and I are both overweight. But when he comes over to my home, he constantly criticizes my food choices. It's so annoying. For instance, uh, he tells me that the potato chips or cookies I'm eating are bad for me and that I shouldn't eat them. Now, uh, you should know that he loves pizza and hamburgers. In fact, he can't get enough of them.

Do you see my point? He's telling me to eat healthy food when he absolutely loves eating junk food. What do I do? Sometimes I just tell him, "You, too." That gets him to shut up, but my response still doesn't excuse me for having a poor diet.

Sample Notes

Thesis Statement: receive criticism from someone who does the same behavior → use the you-too fallacy

Example: professor and bro = overweight

What the Professor's Brother Does:
- criticizes professor's food choices → says don't eat chips or cookies
- loves pizza and hamburgers

What the Professor Does:
- professor says, "You too"
- makes bro shut up → no excuse for poor diet

C

Sample Response 🎧 Q3_02_2

The professor tells the students about his relationship with his older brother. He notes that his brother frequently makes comments about the food he eats. If the professor is eating junk food, his brother will tell him not to have that food because it's unhealthy. The professor mentions that his brother is also overweight and loves to eat junk food such as pizza. To respond to the criticism, the professor sometimes says, "You, too." When the professor responds in that way, he is using the you-too fallacy. This is a logical fallacy that people use when a person criticizing them engages in the same behavior that is being criticized. While the argument is sometimes effective, it still does not excuse the behavior of the person doing it.

iBT Practice Test

Sample Notes — READING

Do actions w/out having to think about them

- implicit memory = recall common actions
- physical acts + chores

Listening Script

Now listen to a lecture on this topic in a psychology class.

M Professor: Memory is a tricky thing. We often have to try hard to remember things like, uh, a phone number or address. But other things are easy to remember because we do them every day. In many cases, they're procedures which require doing actions in a specific order.

For instance, the act of walking is not something you think about as you do it, right? How to walk is so ingrained in your brain that it literally requires no thought. You didn't know how to do it at one point in your life. But you learned to do it and don't need to think about the process of walking now. The same is true for other physical activities, um, such as running and jumping.

And what about other common everyday tasks? Let's see . . . tying your shoes, turning the pages in a book, washing the dishes, cutting vegetables . . . These activities are things you have done for so long and so many times that you no longer have to think about how to do them. They've become implicit memories for you.

Sample Notes LISTENING

Remembering some things is easy

1 **don't need to think about walking**
   - requires no thought → learned to do it long time ago
   - running and jumping = require no thought

2 **common everyday tasks**
   - have done for long time and many times
   - no longer think about doing them = implicit memories

Sample Response 🎧 Q3_02_4

In his talk, the professor states that remembering some things is hard whereas remembering other things requires no conscious thought. He first brings up walking. He says that people have been walking for so long that they don't have to think about how to do it anymore. The same is true for running and jumping. Next, he talks about everyday activities people do, such as washing the dishes and tying their shoes. Because people have done them many times over a long period of time, they don't have to think about the act of doing them. They are implicit memories, which are memories that can be unconsciously remembered. They often have steps involved, but people don't need to think about them since the actions have become ingrained in their memories.

A

Sample Notes

Main Idea of the Passage: employers give rewards to employees

Details: - tangible = money, plaques, certificates, and awards
- intangible = praise, recognition, and positive feedback
- rewards appreciated by workers

B

Listening Script

Now listen to a lecture on this topic in an economics class.

M Professor: Let me explain what I mean by reward power. I believe you'll find this fairly interesting.

My old college roommate is the head of the Sales Department at a local company. A while back, she was told by her boss that she needed to reward her department's best employee one month. Unfortunately for her, her budget was limited. She considered throwing a party for everyone in the department and giving the top employee a certificate at the banquet. But that would be too expensive. Then, she remembered that her company has a monthly online newsletter. She decided to put a picture of the top employee and a short article about his achievements in the newsletter.

In doing that, she solved two problems. Putting the picture and article in the newsletter cost nothing, so, uh, she saved money. Simultaneously, she publicly recognized her top employee. Not only did her team find out about him, but so did the entire company. He was both surprised and pleased by the writeup. And the rest of the team tried harder to make the newsletter in future months.

Sample Notes

Example: professor's old college roommate used intangible reward

Details: - Sales Department head → needed to reward best employee
- couldn't have banquet → not enough money
- put pic and article in newsletter

Results: solved two problems

Details: - no money to put info in newsletter
- recognized employee to entire company
- employee = surprised + pleased

C

During his talk, the professor mentions something his old college roommate did. She needed to give an award to her top salesperson. However, she considered having a party for the entire department, but she lacked enough money. As a result, she put the employee's picture in the company's newsletter and wrote a small article about him. This is an example of reward power. Reward power is a way for managers to give rewards to their employees. These rewards can be tangible and intangible. The professor's roommate gave an intangible reward by publicly recognizing the employee for his performance. The employee was very happy to get acknowledged for his work in such a public manner. The other employees worked harder so that they could get the same recognition in the future, too.

iBT Practice Test

Sample Notes — READING

Price goes up → demand increases

- Giffen good = rare
- usually staples that can't be replaced

Listening Script

Now listen to a lecture on this topic in an economics class.

M Professor: Droughts or periods of intense rain can cause crop failures. These, in turn, result in food shortages, which lead to rising prices for staples. Food shortages always have a, uh, a negative impact on the poor, who rely on staple foods more than others. One strange effect of food shortages is that even though food prices rise, demand for these products increases.

This doesn't appear to make sense, does it? After all, in most situations, when prices go up, demand drops. But that's not always the case for food. Let me describe a historical example . . . uh, the Irish potato famine in the mid-1800s. Back then, potatoes were a staple in Ireland. But during the famine, the Irish potato crop failed, so the price of the few potatoes harvested rose. Most poor Irish couldn't afford to buy other foods, such as meat and fish. Despite the rising prices of potatoes, they were still cheaper than other foods. So poor Irish bought potatoes.

Economist Robert Giffen wrote about instances like this. Basically, what happens in these situations is that a product is widely used and has no affordable substitute. Thus, people pay more even though the price is rising.

Sample Notes — LISTENING

Food shortages → food prices ↑, but demand for staple foods ↑

1. **Irish potato famine in 1800s**
   - potatoes staple in Ireland → potato crop failed
   - potato price rose → was higher than price of other foods
   - poor Irish still bought potatoes

2. **Robert Giffen wrote about this**
   - product is widely used + no affordable substitute
   - pay more despite rising price

The professor lectures about the events involved in the Irish potato famine in the 1800s. According to him, there was a poor potato crop in Ireland. This made the price of potatoes rise very much. Even though the price was high, it was not as expensive as the prices of meat, fish, and other foods. The result was that poor Irish people still bought potatoes despite the rising price. This is an example of a Giffen good. A Giffen good is usually some kind of staple food. It defies the laws of economics because even though the price increases, the demand also increases. Normally, when something's price rises, demand for it decreases. However, Giffen goods are different because there's no substitute for them.

Question 3 #4   p. 90

A

Sample Notes

Main Idea of the Passage: people have expectations during experiments

Details: - may engage in subject expectancy effect
   - have preconceived idea of results → results skewed toward expectations

B

Listening Script

Now listen to a lecture on this topic in a psychology class.

M Professor: I used to work at a pharmaceutical company and conducted tests for new drugs. One problem with doing medical trials was that the people helping with the experiment had, uh, certain expectations for the drugs. They therefore often reported feeling better because they thought they should get better. Naturally, this caused problems with our data.

Once, I tested a new drug which was a pain reliever.

The people taking it understood it was supposed to reduce their pain. As a result, some of them claimed their pain was less than it was before. Pain, as you know, is difficult to measure. It depends on reports by the subjects, which can throw off the data.

What did we do? Well, we conducted a blind trial. We took a large group of people and gave half of them the drug and the other half a placebo, which isn't a drug. But we didn't tell the subjects if they were getting the real drug or not. By not knowing if they had the drug, the subjects' expectations were lowered. This resulted in fewer false expectations being reported, so we got better data.

Example: professor's experience at a pharmaceutical company

What Happened: tested for pain reliever

Details: - people in test knew it was pain reliever

- claimed pain was less than before

- hard to measure pain

How the Professor Solved the Problem: conducted blind trial

Details: - half got drug, and half got placebo → didn't know who got what

- expectations lowered → fewer false expectations

C

Q3_04_2

The professor worked at a pharmaceutical company in the past. There, he conducted tests on medicine being developed. One time, he conducted a test on a pain reliever. Unfortunately, some of the people knew what it was, so they thought they were supposed to get better. They then claimed they felt less pain. This was an example of the subject expectancy effect. It happens when people have expectations for the outcome of a test. They say that what is supposed to happen actually happened to them. This causes problems for the results and the data collected. The professor solved this by giving half of the people the drug and the other half a placebo. The people didn't know who had the drug, so their expectations were lowered. This method provided better data.

iBT Practice Test

Observe activity w/out expending effort

- advantages = rest mind and be relaxed
- disadvantages = lack of understanding if close attention required

Now listen to a lecture on this topic in a psychology class.

W Professor: Your ability to concentrate on a task often depends on its nature. For example, uh, if it's something active which requires close attention, you are more likely to be alert and able to observe and take in everything that's happening. Of course, um, the opposite is true for static situations.

In most static situations, a person's mind doesn't need to concentrate hard. Think about it . . . Watching television, seeing a movie, and reading a book don't require much concentration. This means that your mind doesn't need to take in everything that's going around you as you passively concentrate on the simple task you're doing.

Nevertheless, there are some negative aspects . . . Like, uh, I can see some of you drifting off to sleep in class when I lecture at times. While listening to my lectures may appear to be a static activity, it really isn't. I'm providing you with vital information that should be written down. Your minds need to concentrate to absorb everything I say, or you'll likely do poorly on the test.

1 **static situation = don't concentrate hard**
   - watching TV or movie + reading book = no need to concentrate
   - mind doesn't need to pay close attention

2 **lectures appear static but aren't**
   - professor provides vital info → should write down
   - must concentrate or will do badly on test

Q3_04_4

The professor talks to the students about how much they need to concentrate for static situations. She mentions activities such as watching TV and movies and reading books. She points out that people don't need to focus on them very much. Instead, they can use passive attention. This happens when a person does not have to expend much effort to do a certain activity. However, the professor points out that passive attention is not good for some static situations. For instance, she tells the students that her class is a static situation that requires concentration. Instead of listening passively, the students should take notes and pay close attention. Then, they can do well on her test. In this regard, using passive attention will be a disadvantage for her students.

A

Sample Notes

Main Idea of the Passage: people w/good ideas → make products and license to companies

Details: - sell rights to businesses

     - businesses pay to produce and advertise products

     - creators get royalties

B

Listening Script

Now listen to a lecture on this topic in a marketing class.

M Professor: Lots of people come up with great ideas for products but fail to sell them. Why's that . . . ? Well, for the most part, they lack enough money to invest in production and advertising. As a result, they license their products to others.

Let me explain what I mean here. Many years ago, a man invented a new type of refrigerator motor. It was much more effective than the ones in use at that time. However, he had spent all of his money while making his invention, so he had nothing left for production, advertising, and sales. He then proceeded to offer some big companies the chance to produce the motor for him. After numerous rejections, one company finally agreed.

Soon afterward, the man's motor was used in refrigerators everywhere. They became hot items and were common in people's homes. So, um, while the man lost control of his invention, ultimately, his motor was manufactured and sold on the market. He was paid a nice fee for his invention. I believe he received around five percent of the total sales, which made him a large sum of money.

Sample Notes

Thesis Statement: people come up with great ideas but lack money → license products to others

Example: man made refrigerator motor

Details: - spent money on invention → none left for production, ads, and sales

     - company agreed to produce it

What Happened Afterward: man's motor became hot item

Details: - lost control of invention

     - but made large amount of money

C

Sample Response   Q3_05_2

While lecturing, the professor discusses the invention of a refrigerator motor. He says that a man made it, but he didn't have any money to manufacture and sell it. He convinced a company to sell the product for him. The motor became successful and was used in many refrigerators. This let the man make a lot of money from sales of the motor. The reason he made money was that he sold the license to his product to the manufacturer. Product licensing involves selling the right to produce and sell a product to another person or company. This allows the creator to collect royalties from sales of the product. And the creator doesn't have to worry about manufacturing, marketing, and selling the product.

iBT Practice Test

Sample Notes — READING

Place unusual ads in unexpected places

- effective → surprise and delight people
- think about product + discuss it w/others

Listening Script

Now listen to a lecture on this topic in a marketing class.

M Professor: As you all know, there are numerous ways to advertise products. Common methods include, uh, let's see . . . TV spots, newspaper and magazine pieces, free giveaways, and websites. But there are some other, um, unusual ways in which companies advertise their products.

One such way is to place ads in locations that might not appear obvious at first. Recently, um, I noticed an advertisement in a public bathroom. A sunglasses company had placed ads on the wall over the sinks. The ads were designed to resemble people's faces while they were wearing sunglasses. The bathroom mirrors were the lenses of the glasses. So when I washed my hands, I looked at the ads. Clever, huh?

Some other ads I saw, um, last week, were for a new car. These ads were in a building. The company's cars were painted on the edges around the elevators. When people got on the elevators, it looked like they were getting into the vehicles. Every time I think of it, I remember how ingenious that was. I even took pictures to send to my friends. I'd say both advertisements were well done, wouldn't you?

Unusual ways of advertising

1 **sunglasses ad in public bathroom**
   - mirrors looked like people wearing sunglasses
   - washed hands → looked at ads

2 **car ads in building**
   - painted around elevators
   - got on elevator → looked like was getting in car
   - sent pictures to friends

Sample Response 🎧 Q3_05_4

While lecturing, the professor brings up two advertisements he saw. The first was an ad for sunglasses that was in a public restroom. The ad made it look as if the people looking into the mirror were wearing sunglasses. The second ad was for a car. According to the professor, cars were painted around the elevators in a building. When people got into the elevators, it appeared as though they were getting into the cars instead. Both advertisements are examples of ambient advertising. This is the placement of unique ads in places where they aren't expected. These ads are often creative, so people like them and tell others about them. This is what the professor did since he took pictures of one ad to send to his friends.

Question 3 #6   p. 96

A

Sample Notes

Main Idea of the Passage: some animals regenerate body parts

Details: - tail or leg lost or cut off → grow new one
   - body part usually looks like old on → sometimes smaller or looks different
   - functions like original part

B

Listening Script

Now listen to a lecture on this topic in a zoology class.

W Professor: Take a look at this picture of a starfish . . . Now, uh, look at this one . . . Notice the difference . . . ? The first starfish has four legs while the second one has five legs. Here's the interesting part . . . These pictures show the same starfish.

Let me explain . . . Most starfish have five legs, but some species have up to fifty of them. Sometimes fish or other marine creatures try to eat starfish. They might bite off a leg or two. Fortunately for the starfish, it can regrow missing legs. Most of the time, the new legs look exactly like the old ones. They function perfectly well, too.

Spiders are another type of animal that can regrow missing body parts. As you know, all spiders have eight legs. If a spider loses a leg, it can grow the missing one back. First, it needs to molt by shedding its exoskeleton, uh, you know, its hard outer shell. During the molting process, the spider can regenerate the lost leg. Most of the time, however, the new leg is slightly smaller than the other ones.

Sample Notes

First Example: starfish = has different number of legs

Details: - mostly 5 legs but can have up to 50
   - marine creatures bite off starfish legs
   - starfish can regrow legs → usually look like old ones + function well

Second Example: spiders = regrow missing body parts

Details: - have 8 legs → if lose 1 leg, can grow it back
   - molt by shedding exoskeleton → while molting, regrow lost leg
   - new leg is slightly smaller than old one

C

Sample Response 🎧 Q3_06_2

The professor's lecture is about starfish and spiders. First, she shows the students pictures of a starfish with four legs and one with five. Then, she points out that the pictures show the same starfish. The professor tells the class that starfish sometimes lose legs when fish or other animals try to eat them. Starfish can regrow missing legs though. Their new legs have the same abilities as the previous ones. She then discusses spiders. Spiders that lose legs can regrow their legs when they molt. The new legs are smaller than the original ones though. Both starfish and spiders are capable of regeneration. This involves the regrowing of a body part which is missing. Sometimes the body part is smaller or looks different, but it can be used like normal.

iBT Practice Test

Sample Notes — READING

Hydrothermal vents

- form near underwater volcanoes or where plates drifting apart
- like fountains under water
- shoot hot water w/minerals
- have microecosystems → marine animals live around them

Now listen to a lecture on this topic in a marine biology class.

M Professor: Look at the picture on page 133 in your textbooks, please. Notice how dark smoke is rising from the bottom of the ocean. You may be wondering how that's possible. So, um, let me tell you about black smokers.

Look closely at the picture . . . Notice the chimney-like structure from which the black smoke is rising. That chimney is a black smoker, and the reason the smoke is black is that iron sulfide is being expelled from the chimney. Keep in mind that this particular black smoker is 2,000 meters beneath the surface. Others are even deeper. At those depths, the ocean is extremely cold.

However, the water which black smokers shoot is hot. The reason is that they're a type of hydrothermal vent. We spoke about them previously. Remember . . . ? Some black smokers are so powerful that they can shoot water with minerals in it around sixty meters. What's also interesting is that when the hot minerals mix with the cold water, the minerals solidify. That's how the chimneys form. So the longer a black smoker shoots out minerals, the bigger it gets.

Sample Notes — LISTENING

Black smokers → dark smoke rising from ocean bottom

1 **is chimney-like structure**
   - expels iron sulfide
   - can be 1,000s of meters beneath surface → ocean very cold

2 **shoot hot water → hydrothermal vent**
   - shoot water + minerals 60m
   - minerals solidify when mix w/cold water → forms chimneys

Sample Response 🎧 Q3_06_4

The professor lectures about black smokers. He says they look like chimneys and can be found thousands of meters underwater in the ocean. He mentions that black smokers shoot black smoke containing iron sulfide up to sixty meters. The professor also says that the water coming from black smokers is hot. When the hot water with minerals combines with the cold ocean water, the minerals become solid and form chimneys. The water is hot because black smokers are hydrothermal vents. According to the reading passage, they are underwater geysers that form near volcanoes. They shoot out hot water with minerals and often have their own microecosystems. This results in all kinds of animals living near them even though they are located deep beneath the surface of the ocean.

A

Sample Notes

Main Idea of the Passage: managers can't control everything

Details: - must transfer power to others → delegating authority
   - gives other employee power to make decisions
   - companies operate efficiently + employees get experience

B

Listening Script

Now listen to a lecture on this topic in a business class.

M Professor: I not only teach, but I also have my own company. It's a small consulting firm. Obviously, I'm not always at the office since I come here three days a week. As a result, I have to let my employees be deeply involved in running the company.

It took me a long time to get to this stage though. Initially, I wanted to do everything by myself. I did lots of micromanaging . . . You know, um, I controlled everything and made every decision, um, no matter how big or small. But that was exhausting. And my company started doing poorly. So I gave more power to my employees.

Basically, I delegated authority to a couple of other workers. I let them make more decisions. I let them talk to clients and make deals. Do you know what happened? It worked really well. The employees gained experience and improved at their jobs. My company started making money. In fact, it did so well that I had to hire more workers. I'm a big believer in delegating authority now. Thanks to it, I've got a very successful business.

Sample Notes

Thesis Statement: prof. has company → lets employees be involved in running it

What the Professor Did at First: micromanaged a lot

Details: - controlled everything + made all decisions
   - was exhausting
     company did poorly

What the Professor Did at Later: delegated authority to couple of workers

Details: - talked to clients and made deals → worked well

- employees got experience + improved at jobs
- company made money → hired more workers

C

Sample Response 🎧 Q3_07_2

The professor tells the class about a consulting company that he owns. He mentions that when he first started the company, he made all of the decisions himself. He did that even for small matters. But his company didn't do well, and he was getting tired of all the work. So he gave two of his workers the power to make deals with customers. The workers got better at their jobs and helped his company make money. The professor was even able to expand his company. The professor succeeded by delegating authority. This happens when a manager or person with power gives another individual the right or ability to make decisions. Delegating authority helps companies become more efficient and makes workers better by giving them experience.

iBT Practice Test

Sample Notes — READING

Workers have multiple tasks → must prioritize tasks → which tasks finish first

- most people do time-sensitive tasks
- do this even when other tasks are more important or could have better results
- instead, focus on tasks w/urgent deadlines

Listening Script

Now listen to a lecture on this topic in a business class.

W Professor: When you graduate, the majority of you will find employment somewhere. At your jobs, you'll have various tasks to complete. You'll have to learn to determine which tasks are more important than others. In doing so, be careful not to fall victim to the mere deadline effect.

My old college roommate worked at a pharmaceutical lab. She was doing research on a vaccine. Unfortunately, she didn't prioritize her duties properly. You see, she was constantly getting emails from her supervisors asking for reports and updates. She also had numerous meetings to attend. She spent several hours a day responding to emails and attending meetings.

Because she focused on those two things, which she considered urgent, she didn't spend much time in the lab. Guess what happened . . . Her research got delayed. Then, a team at another pharmaceutical company came out with a vaccine based on the same principles my roommate was working on. That

company got the patent and made billions of dollars. That could have been my friend. But she prioritized the wrong tasks. She should have focused on the less-urgent task with the bigger payout.

Sample Notes — LISTENING

Students will have various tasks at jobs

- be careful about mere deadline effect
1 **roommate worked at pharmaceutical lab**
   - doing vaccine research → didn't prioritize tasks properly
   - answered emails and attended meetings → considered them urgent = research got delayed
   - rival company made vaccine → company made billions of $ → could have been friend

Sample Response 🎧 Q3_07_4

The professor mentions to the students that they should be careful about the mere deadline effect when they get jobs. She uses her old college roommate as an example. Her roommate was trying to develop a vaccine. But she had emails to answer and meetings to attend. Her roommate often chose to focus on the emails and meetings rather than her research. She did that because the emails and meetings were more urgent at the time. Then, another company came out with a vaccine and made a huge amount of money. Because of the mere deadline effect, the professor's roommate failed to develop her own vaccine. The mere deadline effect takes place when people do urgent tasks first instead of focusing on tasks without a deadline but with a bigger payoff.

Question 3 #8   p. 102

A

Sample Notes

Main Idea of the Passage: stress caused by many factors

Details: - include work, school, and personal relationships
- body's reaction to stress = anxiety
- feelings of fear, concern, or worry
- feelings may last long time → anxiety disorder

B

Listening Script

Now listen to a lecture on this topic in a psychology class.

M Professor: During my freshman year of college, I wasn't exactly the best student. I basically skipped tons of classes and didn't care too much. Suddenly, when it was time for final exams, I realized I was in danger of failing several classes.

The week before exams, I started cramming for all of my tests. But there was a big problem. I started to develop some unpleasant symptoms. For instance, I was so worried about failing that my heartbeat was elevated. I don't think my heart has ever beat that fast. My hands also shook all the time. People could tell that I was nervous.

Now, uh, those weren't my only symptoms of anxiety. I got some really bad headaches, so I had trouble concentrating. I felt nauseous at times and even threw up after a couple of meals. I did really poorly that semester, but at least I didn't fail. Afterward, I focused better, studied hard, and eventually became a professor. So I guess you could say that I learned from my feelings of anxiety. It was an unpleasant experience, but, um, the results were eventually positive.

Sample Notes

Thesis Statement: prof. was bad student freshman year → in danger of failing

What Happened: prof. crammed for final exams week before

Details: - developed unpleasant symptoms
- elevated heartbeat → heart beat very fast
- hands shook → nervous
- bad headaches + trouble concentrating + felt nauseous
- did poorly but didn't fail
- later, studied harder and became prof. → learned from feelings of anxiety

C

Sample Response 🎧 Q3_08_2

In his lecture, the professor tells the students a story about when he was a freshman at college. He mentions that he wasn't a good student because he skipped classes and didn't care very much. However, he didn't want to fail his classes, so he began studying hard for his final exams. But he developed several problems. His heart beat very quickly, and his hands shook due to nervousness. He had severe headaches, couldn't concentrate, and threw up sometimes. He mentions that he didn't fail any classes even though he was suffering from anxiety. According to the reading passage, anxiety is caused by stress. It can appear as feelings of fear, concern, or worry. Some people suffer severe problems due to anxiety when it lasts a long time.

iBT Practice Test

Sample Notes — READING

Teamwork = cooperative effort w/2+ people

- work together to achieve shared goal
- focus on strengths + avoid weaknesses
- accomplish goal quickly and efficiently

Listening Script

Now listen to a lecture on this topic in a psychology class.

W Professor: Back when I was a student a couple of decades ago, I used to enjoy working on group projects in my classes. Let me explain why.

When we did group projects, we often had, hmm . . . four or five students in our group. Naturally, all of us had one or two skills which we excelled at. For instance, I was good at doing research. Other students I worked with were excellent public speakers, outstanding at writing or drawing, or fluent in foreign languages. I always made sure that I chose my group's members carefully so that there were no members with overlapping skills.

There was a reason that I did that. I acted that way because we were all able to work well together as a team. We could split up our duties without having any problems. We each did them well, and we worked hard to accomplish our goal. The end result was that I received an A or an A+ on nearly every group project that I did as a university student.

Sample Notes — LISTENING

Prof. enjoyed working on group projects

1 **4 or 5 students in group**
   - 1 or 2 skills excelled at
   - choose group's members carefully → no members w/overlapping skills

2 **worked well together as team**
   - split duties w/out problems
   - worked hard
   - got A or A+ on most group projects

Sample Response 🎧 Q3_08_4

The professor states that she used to enjoy doing group projects as a student. She says she worked in groups of four or five students. Each group member had a particular skill, including being a good researcher, speaking well, and knowing a foreign language. The professor remarks that she made sure her group members didn't have overlapping skills. She did that because it was then easy to divide the work between the group members. All of the members did their assignments well, so she always got good grades. The professor's actions are related to teamwork. This happens when two or more people work together well on a project to achieve a common goal. People rely on teamwork in sports as well as at school and work.

Question 3 #9

p. 105

A

Sample Notes

Main Idea of the Passage: drought = time w/below-average amount of precipitation

Details: - wide range of effects → water levels become lower

- reduce moisture in soil + deplete groundwater supplies
- damage crops + harm people

B

Listening Script

Now listen to a lecture on this topic in an environmental science class.

M Professor: I can't remember the last time we got rain. It's been a while, hasn't it? This drought is definitely causing problems in the region. You know, droughts can be devastating at times. Let me tell you about a couple of times in the past when they helped bring down entire civilizations.

The Mayan Empire once ruled a large area in Mesoamerica. But the Mayans suddenly vanished around, um, 1,200 years ago. Archaeologists have long been confused by this because the Mayans appeared to be thriving when they disappeared. However, some research indicates that there was most likely a period of several years with lower-than-normal precipitation when the Mayans vanished. In all likelihood, the lack of rain caused crop failures, so that made Mayan culture collapse.

Even further back in the past, uh, 4,500 years ago, the Old Kingdom in Egypt came to an end. This was around the time that pyramids were being built. The most likely reason the Old Kingdom ended and the Middle Kingdom began was a lack of rain. Crops couldn't grow, and people couldn't eat. So the Old Kingdom fell, and a new one began.

Sample Notes

Thesis Statement: droughts brought down entire civilizations in past

First Example: Mayan Empire → ruled in Mesoamerica

Details: - vanished around 1,200 years ago → confusing because appeared to be thriving

- research shows were several years with low precipitation
- lack of rain caused crop failures → Mayan civilization collapsed

Second Example: Old Kingdom in Egypt → ended 4,500 years ago

Details: - was time of pyramid building

- Old Kingdom ended due to lack of rain
- no crops, so people couldn't eat

C

Sample Response Q3_09_2

The professor talks about the Mayan Empire and the Old Kingdom in Egypt. He mentions that the Mayan Empire disappeared around 1,200 years ago. He states that archaeologists aren't sure what happened because the Mayans were prospering then. He then comments that it's believed that a drought lasting several years happened. Due to the drought, Mayan civilization fell. The same thing happened to the Old Kingdom in Egypt. Around 4,500 years ago, there was a drought in Egypt. Because crops couldn't grow, people couldn't eat, so the Old Kingdom fell. Both civilizations collapsed because of droughts. A drought is an extended period of time when there is little or no precipitation. Droughts can cause problems such as reducing water levels, harming crops, and causing problems for people.

iBT Practice Test

Sample Notes READING

Water erosion = removal or displacement of ground due to water

- may wash away topsoil
- happens gradually = Grand Canyon took millions of years to form
- happens quickly = floods from heavy rains → dramatic changes to land

Listening Script

Now listen to a lecture on this topic in a geology class.

W Professor: Off the coast of North Carolina and the southern part of Virginia is the Outer Banks. The Outer Banks is comprised mostly of barrier islands, peninsulas, and sandbars. It stretches around 320 kilometers. It's an important region due to its biodiversity and the fact that it helps protect the mainland from storm surges. However, the Outer Banks has been shrinking over the years.

In the past century, some parts of the Outer Banks have decreased in size by more than 400 meters. In other places, approximately 900 meters of land has been reclaimed by the sea. The primary reason for this is the violent storms the region gets.

Hurricanes frequently hit the Outer Banks. These storms can send enormous waves crashing onto shore. These waves wash away sand from the beaches on the Outer Banks. The hurricanes often cause flooding on the islands there, too. During one storm a couple of decades ago, a 600-meter-wide channel was carved out on Hatteras Island, virtually splitting the island in two, by a hurricane. If this erosion continues, someday soon, the Outer Banks may disappear.

Sample Notes — LISTENING

Outer Banks = islands, peninsulas, and sandbars off

North Carolina and Virginia coast

- protects regions from storm surges
- has been shrinking recently
1 **some parts of Outer Banks decreased by 400-900 meters**
   - land reclaimed by sea
   - happens because of violent storms
2 **many hurricanes in Outer Banks**
   - waves wash sand from beaches + cause flooding
   - 600m-wide channel carved out of island in one hurricane = split island in two
   - if erosion continues, Outer Banks may disappear

Sample Response 🎧 Q3_09_4

The professor tells the class about the Outer Banks. It's comprised of numerous barrier islands and other landforms and is located off the coast of North Carolina and Virginia. The Outer Banks protects the mainland from bad weather, but the problem is that the Outer Banks is shrinking. Some places in the Outer Banks have decreased in size by 400 to 900 meters as the ocean has reclaimed the land. Hurricanes are causing most of the damage. Powerful waves wash away sand and cause places in the Outer Banks to be flooded. This is related to water erosion. It happens when water changes the appearance of the land. The reading passage points out that this can happen slowly or quickly. In the Outer Banks, erosion sometimes happens quickly during a single storm.

A

Sample Notes

Main Idea of the Passage: buoyancy → lets ships and boats float on water

Details: - object in water displaces water
   - water of displaced water = more than weight of object → object floats
   - lets metal objects avoid sinking

B

Listening Script

Now listen to a lecture on this topic in a physics class.

W Professor: I find submarines to be some of the most impressive works of technology in the world. I mean, uh, some submarines have crews of 130 or more sailors and can stay underwater for extended periods of time.

One question I often get asked is this . . . How do submarines go down underwater and then head back up to the surface again? Actually, it's simple. Most submarines have compartments called ballast tanks. When the submarine needs to descend, the tanks are filled with water to make it heavier. This creates negative buoyancy, so the submarine goes down.

When the captain wants the submarine to rise to the surface, the submarine needs to be made lighter. So the water is pumped out of the ballast tanks while air is added to them. This creates positive buoyancy, thereby causing the submarine to head upward. It seems complicated, but it's quite a simple procedure as long as you know how much water the submarine displaces. Then, making the sub descend, ascend, or just remain in the same place underwater is simple to do.

Sample Notes

Thesis Statement: submarines → stay underwater for extended periods

How Submarines Descend:

Details: - ballast tanks = compartments in subs
   - fill tanks w/water = heavier sub
   - negative buoyancy → sub goes down

How Submarines Rise:

Details: - need to make sub lighter
   - pump out water + add air = positive buoyancy
   - sub heads upward

C

Sample Response 🎧 Q3_10_2

While lecturing, the professor remarks that she finds submarines to be fascinating due to their ability to travel underwater for a long time. She comments that the principles behind a submarine descending and ascending are easy to understand. Submarines have ballast tanks, which are special compartments. When they need to go down, the tanks get filled with water, which makes them heavier. When submarines need to rise, the tanks are filled with air, which makes them lighter. When submarines are too heavy, they have negative buoyancy, so they sink. When they are light, they have positive buoyancy, so they float. Buoyancy refers to the fact that if an object is lighter than the water it displaces, then it can float. This phenomenon lets ships float on water.

iBT Practice Test

Sample Notes — READING

Levitation = causes something to be suspended in air

- can do this w/magnets → counter effects of gravity
- need multiple magnets to suspend object + keep it stable → prevents it from falling over

Listening Script

Now listen to a lecture on this topic in a physics class.

M Professor: If you ever fly to Shanghai, China, I highly suggest that you make it a point to travel from the airport to the downtown area by train. You'll get to see the sights at speeds of more than 430 kilometers per hour. So you'll make the journey in only about seven or eight minutes.

There are few trains in the world that can move that fast. It is called a maglev train. That's M-A-G-L-E-V. Maglev stands for magnetic levitation. This is how it works. Maglev trains have electromagnets attached to their undersides. The tracks which they move on have coils. There is a constant electric current running through the coils, which allows the train to move along the track.

Thanks to the magnets, the train can, uh, float a few centimeters above the track. Magnetic forces keep it both suspended and balanced, so it doesn't crash. Because it can levitate, there's no friction from touching the tracks. This allows the train to move at incredibly fast speeds while also providing a smooth ride for passengers.

Sample Notes — LISTENING

Shanghai, China → take train downtown

- can travel 430+ km/hr → takes 7 or 8 minutes
1 **maglev train → magnetic levitation**
    - electromagnets on undersides + tracks have coils
    - electric current runs through coils → lets train move on track
2 **magnets let train float above track**
    - magnetic forces = keep train suspended and balanced → doesn't crash
    - no friction from tracks → lets train move incredibly fast

Sample Response 🎧 Q3_10_4

The professor states that it's possible to travel from the Shanghai airport to the downtown area in seven minutes. He says a person can do that by riding on a maglev train, which can move around 430 kilometers per hour. He then remarks that maglev stands for magnetic levitation. A maglev train has electromagnets on its bottom, and it travels on tracks that have coils that transmit electricity. The magnets can make the train levitate a few centimeters above the tracks. This lets the train move very quickly because of a lack of friction. This happens due to the principle of magnetic levitation. Magnets are capable of defeating the force of gravity and making something be suspended in the air while remaining stable.

Question 4 #1   p. 115

A

Listening Script

Listen to part of a lecture in a zoology class.

M Professor: Rhesus monkeys live in colonies consisting of a few dozen to a few hundred animals. They have a strict social hierarchy which they follow. For instance, um, when monkeys are born, the mothers allow younger females to care for the babies.

There are a few advantages to this. One is that the mothers can do other tasks while the younger females are caring for their babies. These tasks include, uh . . . let's see . . . foraging for food and grooming. Having enough time to do these tasks helps the mothers survive. Why is that . . . ? Well, they remain strong and healthy, so the mothers can rear their babies until they're ready to survive on their own. Oh, in case you're curious, the female babysitters aren't alone. While the mothers are doing various tasks, other adults watch the young females. They make sure the newborn monkeys aren't harmed.

A second advantage is that young female rhesus monkeys get to practice their mothering skills. Zoologists observing young females have noticed that they're intensely curious about newborns. They want to touch the babies, hold them, and groom them once their mothers leave them unattended. This is most likely an innate desire to be a mother. Well, uh, whatever it is, they learn how to be good mothers in the future. And that helps rhesus monkey colonies thrive since the babies are taken care of.

Sample Notes

Main Topic: rhesus monkey baby rearing

Main Idea: young females care for babies of mothers → several advantages

First Advantage: mothers can do other tasks

Details: - help mothers raise young to survive

      - help them stay strong and healthy

      - other adults watch young females → make sure newborns not harmed

Second Advantage: young females practice mothering skills

Details: - young females curious about newborns → innate desire

      - can learn to be good mothers in future

B

Sample Response 🎧 Q4_01_2

The professor tells the class that the mothers of newborn rhesus monkeys allow young females to look after them sometimes. He believes there are two advantages to this. The first is that the mothers get time to do activities other than raising their babies. According to the professor, they are able to search for food, rest, and groom themselves. He points out that this lets the mothers survive since they can stay both strong and healthy. The second advantage he mentions concerns the young female monkeys. The professor notes that these monkeys are interested in the newborns and want to look after them. As a result, the young females gain valuable mothering skills, which they can use later in life when they become mothers.

iBT Practice Test

Listening Script

Listen to part of a lecture in a zoology class.

M Professor: The giraffe is an herbivore which has evolved to have special features that help it eat. First, of course, is that every giraffe has a very long neck. Second are the various special features of the giraffe's mouth. Both of them provide advantages to giraffes while they're feeding.

Let me start by talking about the giraffe's neck. It allows the giraffe to reach plant matter located high up in trees. The tallest giraffes can feed on leaves growing five meters above the ground. The only other animals that can do that are the largest elephants. The giraffe's height advantage therefore gives it access to food that virtually no other animals can eat. As a result, the lack of competition gives the giraffe more food to eat and a greater chance to survive.

Now, uh, what about the giraffe's mouth . . . ? The animal's favorite food comes from the acacia tree. Yet these trees have long, sharp thorns, so eating the leaves is a problem for most animals. Fortunately for the giraffe, its tongue is coated with fleshy protrusions. These protect its tongue from harmful thorns. Giraffes also produce thick saliva. The saliva covers any thorns the giraffe happens to swallow, so its internal organs don't get harmed. These two features help the giraffe get access to food most animals can't eat.

1 **neck → can reach plant matter 5 meters above ground**
   - only elephants can reach that high
   - has access to food other animals can't get
   - eats more so better chance to survive
2 **loves acacia tree leaves → sharp thorns**
   - tongue has fleshy protrusions – protect from thorns
   - thick saliva – covers thorns giraffe swallows → organs not harmed

Q4_01_4

The professor states that the giraffe has developed two special features which help it when it eats. The first is its very long neck. It enables the giraffe to eat leaves five meters above the ground. The professor claims that only a few elephants can reach that high. The result is that the giraffe has a food source almost no other animals can access. The second feature is the giraffe's mouth. The giraffe likes eating acacia tree leaves, but that tree is protected by sharp thorns. The giraffe's tongue is protected as well though, so the thorns don't harm its tongue. And if the giraffe swallows a thorn, saliva in its mouth surrounds the thorn. That prevents the thorn from damaging the giraffe's organs.

Question 4 #2
p. 118

A

Listen to part of a lecture in an economics class.

W Professor: In business, it's necessary to build rapport with your clients. By that, uh, I mean establishing good relationships with them. The reason is that once you attract clients, you need to keep them to provide you with repeat business. There are several ways you can build rapport. I'd like to tell you about two of them now.

First, treat your clients with kindness and respect and show them that you care about both them and their concerns. Some ways to do this include, uh, returning calls and emails promptly, offering customer service all day long, listening to complaints, and acting on clients' suggestions. One example is a credit card company having customer service representatives on call all the time. After all, credit card problems can happen anytime and anywhere. By providing these kinds of services, a company can show its customers that it cares and isn't just after their money.

Another way to build rapport is to offer incentives to clients so that they remain customers. Incentives can include, hmm . . . discounts on products, access to new products before the general public can buy them, and benefits for long-term customers. I think a perfect example is airlines that offer extra mileage to frequent long-distance travelers. The discount cards which many coffee shops and fast-food establishments give to their customers are another example. These special deals encourage customers to return for more business and improve the companies' relationships with their customers.

Main Topic: building rapport with clients

Main Idea: building rapport = important to get repeat business

First Way: treat clients w/kindness and respect → show care for them

Details: - credit card companies = 24-hour customer service reps
   - can solve problems for customer

Second Way: offer incentives to clients → remain customers

Details: - discounts, early access to new products, and benefits
   - airlines = extra mileage for frequently fliers
   - coffee shops and fast-food places = discount cards
   - encourage repeat business

B

Q4_02_2

The subject of the professor's lecture is how to build rapport with customers to guarantee repeat business. The professor covers two ways that businesses can do this. Firstly, she states that customers need to be shown that businesses care about them and their problems. This can be done through good customer service. She gives an example of a credit card company that has a twenty-four-hour hotline for its customers. Secondly, she states that businesses need to give their customers incentives to continue being customers. She provides two examples of this. The first is airlines giving extra mileage to frequent fliers. And the second is coffee shops and restaurants providing discount cards to customers. According to her, both of these methods will improve rapport between businesses and customers.

Listen to part of a lecture in an economics class.

M Professor: Every company needs to grow to avoid becoming stagnant and, uh, possibly failing. Growth typically requires investment by the company so that it can expand its operations. Investment funds can come from internal or external sources.

Internal investments mainly come from a company's profits. Basically, a company takes some of its profits and invests them in the business. It might use the money to buy new equipment, to expand existing structures or to buy new ones, and, um, to develop new ideas and procedures. The main advantage of internal investment is that the company owners can maintain control of the business and don't have to deal with outside influence. The main disadvantage is that the amount of money invested is limited by the company's profits.

There's no limit on external investments though. They mostly come from bank loans and private investors. Regarding bank loans, companies with sound business practices can get them easily. But loans must be repaid with interest. So, uh, they are expensive in the long run. As for private investors, companies can get large amounts of cash rather quickly. But the firms must give up some amount of control. And they have to pay dividends to stockholders, so they can't keep all the profits that they make.

Sample Notes

Companies must grow → need investment

1　**internal investments → from company's profits**
　- invest in business → buy equipment, expand structure, and develop new ideas and procedures
　- maintain control of business
　- investment amount limited by profits

2　**external investments → from bank loans and private investors**
　- easy to get loan but must pay back w/interest
　- get lots of money from private investors → give up control + pay dividends

Sample Response 🎧 Q4_02_4

The professor tells the class about internal investments and external investments. He points out that companies need to grow to survive, so they often invest money to do that. First, he covers internal investments. These investments are funded by the company's own money. They're paid for by the company's profits. This allows the company to maintain control over its actions, but it cannot invest more money than it actually has. Second, he describes external investments. These are funds that come from outside the company. The professor mentions bank loans and money from private investors. These are beneficial because they can provide large amounts of money. But bank loans must be repaid while investors want control of the company or dividends paid to them.

Question 4 #3　　　　　　　　p. 121

A

Listening Script

Listen to part of a lecture in a psychology class.

W Professor: Making plans is usually necessary, but, well, excessive planning can result in several problems. By excessive planning, uh, I mean that a plan has so many details that it's too rigid. Here are a couple of examples of what I mean.

When I was a university student, I decided to make my life easier by planning everything in detail. I planned, uh, my assignments, my study time, my free time, and just about everything else I had to do. But my plans never worked. Small things always popped up to ruin them. For instance, someone would call me while I was studying . . . The weather would be bad when I wanted to travel . . . I would get sick before an exam. These interruptions frustrated me so much that I gave up on making excessive plans.

Another issue is that we sometimes don't leave enough time for certain activities in our plans. Last week, one of my colleagues wanted me to review a paper he had written. I thought it would take two hours, so I planned to do it on Saturday morning before I spent the rest of the day doing a variety of activities with my family. I also intended to go hiking with my family on Sunday. But reading the paper took much longer than that. I had to do research and take notes while reading it. As a result, my weekend plans were completely ruined.

Sample Notes

Main Topic: excessive planning

Main Idea: excessive planning = plan w/too many details → rigid

First Example: made detailed plans in university

Details: - small things always ruined plans → phone calls, bad weather, sickness

　　　- frustrated by interruptions → gave up planning

Second Example: don't leave enough time in plans

Details: - colleague asked to review paper

- thought would take 2 hours → do in morning
- made plans for rest of weekend
- took too long to review → ruined weekend plans

B

Sample Response Q4_03_2

The professor tells the class that excessive planning often results in problems. She then provides two personal examples showing the students what she means. First, she talks about her personal life when she was a university student. She says that she made plans for all kinds of situations. However, something always happened which caused her plans to be interrupted. She comments that she quit making detailed plans because of that. Second, the professor talks about a colleague who asked her to read a paper. She thought it would take a couple of hours, so she made excessive weekend plans. However, reading the paper took a very long time. As a result, her weekend plans had to change. She wasn't able to do the activities with her family that she had planned.

iBT Practice Test

Listening Script

Listen to part of a lecture in a psychology class.

W Professor: Many people have things to do but little or no desire to do them. They therefore need something to motivate them. This can come from within themselves or from an outside source. We call internal sources intrinsic motivation and external sources extrinsic motivation.

A lot of times, people do activities because they enjoy them or get pleasure from them. This is what intrinsic motivation is. My brother's hobby is photography. He carries his camera with him all the time so that he can take pictures. He also travels to various places in order to take pictures of people or scenery. He doesn't take pictures to earn money or to become famous. Instead, he does it solely because it's fun. That's intrinsic motivation.

What about extrinsic motivation? Well, this typically involves some kind of a tangible reward. For instance, in the future, you're all going to graduate and get jobs. Many of you won't enjoy your jobs, but you'll still go to work every day. Why . . . ? That's easy. Money. That's a major type of extrinsic motivation. Of course, uh, some of you will work hard to get a promotion or a transfer overseas. Another example is professional athletes. They exercise hard every day to win games and, for many of them, to become rich and famous. Those are all extrinsic motivations.

Sample Notes

Need motivation to do activities

1 **intrinsic motivation → do because enjoy or get pleasure**
   - bro's hobby = photography
   - always has camera → travels to take pictures
   - doesn't make money or want to be famous
   - takes pictures because is fun

2 **extrinsic motivation = tangible reward for doing**
   - have job → don't enjoy but work for money, promotion, or transfer
   - professional athletes → work out hard
   - want to win games + be rich and famous

Sample Response Q4_03_4

The professor lectures to the class on intrinsic motivation and extrinsic motivation. She talks about intrinsic motivation first. She states that this type of motivation is based on doing an activity because the person enjoys it. The professor uses her brother as an example. She mentions that he likes photography. He always takes his camera with him, and he loves traveling to take pictures. He doesn't make money from it. It's just his hobby. As for extrinsic motivation, this is a type of motivation where a person is rewarded for doing something. The professor comments that the students will work after graduation because they want money or promotions. She also remarks that professional athletes train a lot to win games and to become wealthy and famous.

Question 4 #4   p. 124

A

Listening Script

Listen to part of a lecture in a meteorology class.

M Professor: When the temperature falls below freezing, the ice in rivers and lakes often freezes. Parts of the oceans sometimes freeze, too. The ice normally freezes in flat sheets, but it makes strange formations at times. Two of them are ice circles and pancake ice. Both are round in shape but get created in different ways.

The motion of swiftly moving water forms ice circles. They typically form on rivers with eddies, which are places where the water rotates. Here's what happens . . . The motion of water breaks a piece of ice from a larger sheet of ice. As the water swirls, the piece of ice bumps into other pieces of ice as it goes around and around, so the edges are smoothed into the shape of a circle. Ice circles can appear alone or in clusters.

Most are small, but there have been reports of some being up to fifteen meters in diameter.

As for pancake ice, it forms on the ocean. When ice crystals form in the water, they come together into sheets called grease ice. That's G-R-E-A-S-E. But the ocean is rough due to waves, so the grease ice breaks up into smaller pieces. While they bump and grind against one another, they start resembling flat disks, uh, like pancakes. This is called, unsurprisingly, pancake ice. Pancake ice can amass in large amounts because the individual pieces are so small. Here, uh, I think I've got some pictures of it.

Sample Notes

Main Topic: ice formations

Main Idea: frozen water in rivers, lakes, and oceans → strange formations

First Type: ice circles → formed by swiftly moving water

Details: - form on rivers w/eddies

- water motion breaks off ice piece

- ice moves in circle → hits other ice pieces → sides smoothed into circle

- can appear alone or in clusters

Second Type: pancake ice → forms on ocean

Details: - grease ice breaks into small pieces → bump against one another

- look like flat disks → pancake ice

- very small so appear in large amounts

B

Sample Response Q4_04_2

In his lecture, the professor discusses ice circles and pancake ice. These are two types of ice formations which are a bit similar to each other. First, the professor talks about ice circles. According to him, they mostly appear on rivers where there are eddies with rotating water. Basically, a large sheet of ice breaks and moves in circles. It hits other pieces of ice, so its edges get transformed into a circular shape. Ice circles are usually small but may have diameters of fifteen meters. Pancake ice forms on oceans instead of on rivers. When ice forms on the ocean, it often gets broken into small pieces because of the action of waves. The ice pieces bump into one another and develop shapes that are like pancakes.

iBT Practice Test

Listening Script

Listen to part of a lecture in a geology class.

W Professor: In deserts around the world, there are singing sand dunes. Now, uh, they don't sing songs, of course, but they do produce loud sounds in different ranges. How they make sound had been a mystery for many years until scientists finally figured it out.

First, it was learned that the sizes of the grains of sand in a dune are important because sound is produced when they move against one another. Each time the grains hit, they produce a tiny sound wave. When masses of sand move, there are enormous numbers of collisions, so they produce loud sounds. If the grains in a dune are all the same size, they'll produce the same sound over and over. But grains of different sizes produce different sounds. In one experiment, a dune with uniform grains produced a constant sound at 105 hertz. Another dune with different-sized grains produced nine different sounds ranging from ninety to 150 hertz.

Next, the speed of the falling grains influences the sounds they create. You see, uh, as they fall, the number of sound-producing collisions varies. Large grains move more slowly than small grains because they have to move more as they go around one another. Producing fewer collisions than small grains, large grains make different sounds. Now that I've explained that, let's listen to some singing sand dunes.

Sample Notes

Sand dunes make singing sounds

1 **sizes of grains of sand important**
   - sound produced when move against one another
   - lots of sands moves → many collisions → loud sounds
   - different sizes of grains = different sounds

2 **speed of falling grains important**
   - large grains fall slowly → produce few collisions
   - small grains fall quickly → produce more collisions and different sounds

Sample Response Q4_04_4

The professor discusses singing sand dunes in her lecture. She says that scientists were able to identify two reasons why they made singing sounds. The first reason concerns the sizes of the grains of sand. According to the professor, when grains of sand hit one another, they make sounds. Because sand dunes are so large, they can make loud sounds. When grains of sand are the same size, they make the same sounds. When they are different sizes, they create different sounds. Next, how fast the grains of sand move determines the types of sounds they make. The professor says that small grains move faster than large ones. As a result, small grains have more collisions, so they make different sounds than large grains, which have fewer collisions.

A

Listen to part of a lecture in an anthropology class.

W Professor: The discovery of how to make fire was crucial for prehistoric humans. How to make and use fire was discovered approximately one million years ago. That was during the early Stone Age. It resulted in two huge benefits.

First, our early ancestors were able to cook and preserve their food. Prior to discovering fire, humans ate raw food. Cooked food is easier for the body to digest though. In addition, prehistoric humans became able to eat more food, such as, uh, plant roots and grains. Those foods are difficult to eat unless they are cooked. I mean, uh, who wants to eat uncooked rice? Cooking also destroyed bacteria and preserved food longer. This ensured a larger food supply. Finally, prehistoric humans learned to dry meat by fires. This preserved food for a long time. So early humans could survive during times when food was scarce.

Fire played a role in hunting, too. It enabled our early ancestors to make better hunting tools. For example, um, they learned how to harden spear points in fires. They also learned to split stone by heating it in fires. They then used the split stone to make axes and other sharp tools. These weapons made it easier to kill animals. Ah, and some humans used fire when they hunted. By lighting fires in certain places, they were able to force animals toward large hunting parties. That made hunting less difficult.

Sample Notes

Main Topic: the fire revolution

Main Idea: humans discovered how to make fire one million years ago

First Benefit: cook and preserve food

Details: - ate raw food before fire
- cooked food = easier to digest
- could eat more food if cooked
- cooking → killed bacteria + preserved food = bigger food supply
- dried food by fires → preserved food

Second Benefit: used fire for hunting

Details: - made hunting tools w/fire → hardened spear points + split stones
- easier to kill animals
- lit fires in places → forced animals toward hunting parties

B

Sample Response 🎧 Q4_05_2

The professor lectures on the discovery of fire by humans a million years ago. She remarks that it had two primary benefits. The first concerned food. Thanks to fire, humans didn't have to eat raw food. By cooking food, they could digest it better, and they could also eat a wider variety of food. This included roots and grains. After cooking food and drying it by fires, humans could preserve their food. This helped them when there wasn't much food to eat. She also talks about how humans used fire for hunting. They made spear points hard in fires and split stone with it. Then, they used those stones to make weapons. This made hunting easier. They also used fire to drive animals to other hunters to kill the animals.

iBT Practice Test

Listening Script

Listen to part of a lecture in a marketing class.

M Professor: Most businesses need to advertise to sell their products. To know how they should advertise, they should consider the primary and secondary demands for the goods and services they sell.

Primary demand encompasses the entire range of products and services. This includes all the brands for a specific product or service. Let's take, um, cars as an example. For primary demand, we must consider the entire car industry, not just one or two companies. We therefore look at general patterns for what people want in new cars. Safety is something which most people want in their cars. As a result, companies tailor their ads to focus on the safety of their vehicles. That's how primary demand works in advertising.

What about secondary demand? It refers to the demand for certain products. Advertisers study it to understand why people are attracted to certain brands. Then, they can produce ads that focus on what people particularly like about those brands. Again, let's think of cars. Ferrari is a popular maker of sports cars. People who buy Ferraris want sleek, beautiful, fast cars. Therefore, the company's ads should emphasize speed and design. But Ford SUVs are family cars. Thus, advertisers should stress the cargo space, gas efficiency, and affordable prices of those vehicles.

Businesses → advertise to sell products

1 **primary demand → entire range of products and services**
   - all brands for product or service
   - cars → consider entire car industry
   - look at general patterns for what people want
   - safety → make ads about safety of cars

2 **secondary demand → demand for certain products**
   - understand why people like brands
   - Ferrari → sports car → ads focus on speed and design
   - Ford → family cars → ads focus on cargo space, fuel efficiency, and affordable prices

🎧 Q4_05_4

The professor mentions that primary demand and secondary demand are both important to advertisers. He starts by defining primary demand. It covers every brand for particular goods or services. He uses the car industry as an example. The professor comments that most people are interested in safe cars no matter which company they are buying from. Therefore, advertisers should be sure to stress the safety of their cars in commercials. Next, the professor defines secondary demand. This is the demand for specific goods or services. He again talks about cars. But this time he mentions the specific brands Ferrari and Ford. He points out that Ferrari ads should emphasize the sports-car nature of the vehicles. However, Ford SUV ads should focus on other aspects of those vehicles.

Question 4 #6   p. 130

A

Listen to part of a lecture in a sociology class.

W Professor: Lately, our state has been constructing a large number of toll roads connecting major cities and suburbs. Now, uh, some people are complaining about them. But I'm not one of those individuals. In fact, I rather like toll roads because they provide several benefits.

One of those benefits is that they are paid for by the people who use them. Think about it . . . In our city, the roads are all free. You know, everyone can drive on them. But the city uses our tax money to pay to build the roads and to repair them. It doesn't matter if you don't use the roads or don't even own a car. You're paying for those roads if you're a taxpayer.

Toll roads, on the other hand, only receive funding from the people who drive on them. To me, that makes sense. We ought to let the people who drive on the roads pay for them.

There's a second benefit to toll roads. Many people don't want to pay to use them. As a result, these drivers find alternative free routes to their destinations. That means that toll roads are often not busy. So people don't have to worry about traffic jams. I live in the suburbs, and a toll road is being built near my place. I'll definitely take it to work every day. The reduced traffic should make my commute to school much faster.

Main Topic: toll roads

Main Idea: toll roads = provide several benefits

First Benefit: paid for by people who use them

Details: - roads free in city → city uses tax money to build and repair roads
   - all taxpayers pay for roads even if don't have car
   - toll roads = receive funding from people who drive on them → makes sense

Second Benefit: many people don't want to pay for toll roads

Details: - find alternative free routes → toll roads often not busy
   - no traffic jams on toll roads
   - prof. will have faster commute to school on toll road

B

🎧 Q4_06_2

The professor lectures about toll roads. She says her state is building some to connect cities with suburbs. She mentions that some people dislike them, but she likes them. One reason is that the funding for toll roads comes from the people who drive on them. She says that all taxpayers in her city contribute to the building and the repairing of roads there even if they don't drive. She then points out the people who use toll roads are the ones who pay for them. She thinks that's logical. The other reason she states is that many people don't want to pay to drive on toll roads. They therefore don't have traffic jams. So her commute to work will be faster when she drives on a toll road.

iBT Practice Test

Listen to part of a lecture in a sociology class.

M Professor: I'm sure everyone is familiar with the big debate going on in the city. The local professional baseball team wants a new stadium. And the team wants the city to pay for it. If that happens, the city will increase the sales tax for the next few years because the stadium's price is estimated at half a billion dollars.

Public financing of sports stadiums and arenas has become popular recently. There are a few advantages. But I'd like to focus on the drawbacks. One is something I already mentioned. The local sales tax rate will increase. It's already seven percent, so it would probably rise to nine percent. That might not seem like much, but it adds up over the course of a year. In addition, the mayor claims the increase will be temporary. Well, uh, that's what politicians always say. But taxes never seem to go down. They just keep going up and up.

Another problem with public financing is that the team which will benefit is privately owned. And the owner happens to be a billionaire. You know what . . . ? He should build his own stadium. He doesn't need the city to pay for it. I find it offensive that an extremely wealthy man wants people to pay for something that he'll earn money from. That's wrong, and I hope the people of the city vote against the proposal to raise taxes for the stadium.

Sample Notes

Drawbacks to public financing of sports stadiums

1 **local sales tax will increase**
   - rise from 7% to 9% → adds up over course of year
   - mayor claims increase is temporary
   - prof. says taxes never go down → always go up

2 **public financing will benefit privately owned team**
   - owner is billionaire → can build own stadium
   - doesn't need city to pay for it
   - prof. offended wealthy man wants people to pay for stadium

Sample Response 🎧 Q4_06_4

The professor talks to the students about a proposal to publicly finance a new stadium for a professional baseball team. The professor is opposed to this proposal for two reasons. The first reason is that the professor thinks the local sales tax will go up. He notes that it's seven percent now and would likely increase to nine percent if the proposal passed. Even though the mayor claims the tax increase will be temporary, the professor doesn't believe

the mayor. The second reason is that the team's owner is very wealthy. As a billionaire, the owner can afford to pay for the construction of the stadium himself. The professor thinks it's wrong for local residents to pay for something another person will make money from.

Question 4 #7 p. 133

A

Listening Script

Listen to part of a lecture in a zoology class.

M Professor: All life on the planet needs water to survive. We humans need to drink plenty of water each day, and so do many other animals. Not all animals get the water their bodies require by drinking it though. Let me tell you about a couple of unique animals. They get water in, hmm . . . creative ways.

This here . . . is a picture of the thorny devil lizard. It can be found in various dry parts of Australia. Now, uh, do you see those spines all over its body? Those spines—along with the lizard's skin—are able to absorb dew and water from puddles and other sources and draw it into the lizard's body. If the lizard can't get enough water that way, it uses another method. The lizard buries itself in sand and extracts moisture from it. Pretty cool, huh?

Here's another interesting animal. This . . . animal on the screen is the Mojave Desert tortoise. It's native to the Mojave Desert in the American Southwest. This tortoise survives on fewer than two liters of water a year. Fortunately for it, the tortoise has a huge bladder. Its kidneys are capable of reabsorbing the urine in this bladder multiple times and using it to rehydrate the tortoise's body. In this way, the tortoise can survive the harsh conditions of the desert, where it rarely rains.

Sample Notes

Main Topic: how animals get water

Main Idea: all animals need water → not all drink it though

First Example: thorny devil lizard → lives in dry parts of Australia

Details: - spines on body absorb dew + water in puddles
   - water drawn into lizard's body
   - can bury self in sand and extract moisture from it

Second Example: Mojave Desert tortoise → lives in American Southwest

Details: - survives on fewer than 2 liters of water/year

- has huge bladder → kidneys reabsorb urine multiple times = rehydrates body
- can survive harsh conditions in desert

B

Q4_07_2

In the professor's lecture, he comments that all animals need water to live. He says that a lot of animals just drink water, but others satisfy their water needs in other ways. He talks about how the thorny devil lizard and Mojave Desert tortoise get water. As for the thorny devil lizard, it uses the spines on its body and its skin to absorb water. It can take water from puddles and even from dew into its body. Sometimes it even removes water from sand in the desert. In addition, the Mojave Desert tortoise recycles its own urine. The tortoise's kidneys are able to take urine from its bladder and use it to provide the water the animal needs to survive in the dry desert.

iBT Practice Test

Listen to part of a lecture in a zoology class.

W Professor: We all know that ants make nests in the ground. I'm sure you've all seen anthills while walking in the forest or, uh, even in your yard at home. Not all ants build nests in the ground though. Some make nests in different places.

One common ant is the carpenter ant. Can you guess from its name where it likes to build its nests . . . ? That's right. It prefers to build nests in wood. Carpenter ants can frequently be found living in rotting tree trunks. Carpenter ant nests may also be found in wooden posts, tree branches, and even timber used to make houses and buildings with. Basically, uh, the ants chew through the wood to hollow it out. Now, uh, they aren't like termites, so they don't eat the wood. They just make their homes in it.

Weaver ants, which mostly live in Africa and Asia, don't make nests in the ground either. Instead, they build nests in trees. Here's what they do . . . First, they get some leaves. Then, they use their own larvae, which can make silk. Adult weaver ants take the sticky silk from the larvae and glue the leaves together with it. Some nests have just a couple of leaves attached to each other while bigger nests have large numbers of them. The larvae are then placed inside the nest, and the adults watch them until they grow up.

Not all ants build nests in ground

1 **carpenter ant = builds nests in wood**
   - lives in rotting tree trunks or posts, branches, and timber
   - ants chew through wood → hollow it out

2 **weaver ants = build nests in trees**
   - get sticky silk from own larvae
   - glue leaves together with silk → can have nests w/many leaves
   - put larvae in nests → adults watch

Q4_07_4

In her lecture, the professor discusses carpenter ants and weaver ants. She tells the students that those two ants don't build nests in the ground. Instead, they build nests in other places. As for carpenter ants, she comments that they make nests in wood. They prefer rotting tree trunks, but they may make nests in other kinds of wood. According to the professor, carpenter ants don't eat wood. All they do is chew wood to hollow it out to make their homes. Next, the professor covers weaver ants. These ants make their nests with leaves. They use weaver ant larvae, which can make sticky silk. The silk is used to glue the leaves together. Some weaver ant nests have just two leaves whereas others have many.

Question 4 #8 p. 136

A

Listen to part of a lecture in a marketing class.

M Professor: Celebrity endorsements are when a famous person, such as a professional athlete, a movie star, or a musician, promotes a product or a service. Sometimes these endorsements can be spectacular successes. For instance, Michael Jordan made billions of dollars for Nike by promoting basketball shoes. Nevertheless, celebrity endorsements have some disadvantages.

One is that people's perceptions of certain celebrities can change suddenly. This summer, a famous movie actor was arrested. You remember that, don't you? Well, that actor was the primary spokesman for a luxury car brand. He was constantly on television commercials, and you could see ads with him on the Internet, too. Guess what happened . . . Sales of that luxury car have plummeted more than sixty percent since his arrest. After all, um, nobody wants to be associated with a criminal.

Another drawback is that some celebrity endorsements can be expensive. A few years ago, a soft drink company signed a deal with a pop singer to advertise its colas. The singer earned more than ten million dollars a year for that endorsement. Now that particular company wound up making money on the deal. But it wasn't very profitable. And the main reason was that the payments to the singer were so high. So, um, sales improved, but the company didn't renew the singer's contract because it was spending too much money on him.

Sample Notes

Main Topic: celebrity endorsement

Main Idea: celebrity endorsements = famous person promotes product or service

First Drawback: people's perceptions change

Details: - famous actor arrested → spokesman for luxury car brand
- was on many ads
- sales of car down 60% → don't want to be associated w/criminal

Second Drawback: celebrity endorsements = expensive

Details: - pop singer advertised colas → earned more than $10 million/year
- company made $ but wasn't too profitable
- spent too much money on singer → didn't renew contract

B

Sample Response Q4_08_2

The professor lectures to the class on celebrity endorsements. He points out that they have some advantages, but he also says that they have some drawbacks. He discusses two disadvantages in detail. The first is that the way people think about certain celebrities can change quickly. He talks about a singer who endorsed a luxury car brand. When the singer was arrested, sales of the luxury car declined sixty percent. The professor remarks that people don't want anything to do with criminals. Next, the professor mentions a singer who advertised for a cola company. The singer made several million dollars each year, and that was a problem for the company. Because it paid the singer so much, it couldn't make enough of a profit.

iBT Practice Test

Listening Script

Listen to part of a lecture in a marketing class.

W Professor: Let's talk about brand equity for a moment. First, what is brand equity? That's easy. It's the extra value which a company gets from the name of its

product as opposed to a generic product. Think about something like this. Would you rather take a generic aspirin or a Tylenol? Lots of people would choose Tylenol since it's a name which they know and trust. That's brand equity.

So . . . how can a company build brand equity? There are many ways. I'll tell you about two now. First, a company can build greater awareness of its brand. That way, um, more customers know about it. It can improve awareness by, let's see . . . providing outstanding customer service, by maintaining email lists to give customers updates, and by using social media sites to share news with customers. All those actions can improve people's awareness of a company.

A company can also let people know what its brand stands for. What do I mean by that . . . ? Well, when you think of the car manufacturer Toyota, what comes to mind? For most people, it's quality, reliable, and inexpensive cars. Those three things are what the Toyota brand stands for. Companies need to communicate to their customers—and potential customers—what they stand for. If people like what the brand represents, they're more likely to purchase it.

Sample Notes

Brand equity = extra value company gets from name of product

1 **build greater awareness of brand = build brand equity**
   - make more customers know about it
   - outstanding customer service, email lists, and social media sites

2 **let people know what brand stands for**
   - Toyota brand = quality, reliable, inexpensive cars
   - communicate to customers and potential customers what companies stand for
   - like what brand represents → more likely to purchase

Sample Response Q4_08_4

In her lecture, the professor mentions brand equity. She says it's the value a company gets from the name of a product it sells as opposed to selling a generic product. She mentions two ways that companies can build brand equity. First, she states that companies can make more people aware of their products. She mentions that businesses can be good at customer service, can have email lists, and can use social media to help people learn more about their products. The second way to build brand equity is to let people know what a brand represents. She says that most people think of Toyota cars as well made, reliable, and cheap. Companies must let their customers and future customers know what their brands stand for to improve sales.

Question 4 #9 p. 139

A

Listening Script

Listen to part of a lecture in a zoology class.

M Professor: Do you know what the world's most effective predator is? No, it's not the great white shark or the lion or even the wolf. It's . . . the dragonfly. Yes, the dragonfly. This insect has a success rate of around ninety-five percent when it hunts. It's successful for two primary reasons.

The first of these is visual. Take a look at the dragonfly's eyes in this picture here . . . Do you see how huge they are? The dragonfly's eyes give it a virtual 360-degree view of the world. That makes spotting prey, such as mosquitoes, relatively easy. In addition, the dragonfly's compound eyes allow it always to stay focused on its prey. So even while the dragonfly is performing aerial twists and turns as it pursues an animal, it keeps a steady eye on whatever it's hunting.

The second reason is mental. The dragonfly has an amazing ability to predict what route its prey will take when it attempts to escape. It can then move in that direction even before its prey flies that way. In this way, the dragonfly is acting rather than reacting, which is what its prey is doing. Thus the dragonfly is just a bit faster than its prey. As a result, most of the time, it is able to catch, kill, and eat whatever it is pursuing.

Sample Notes

Main Topic: Dragonfly hunting methods

Main Idea: dragonfly = world's most effective predator → 95% success rate when hunts

First Reason: has huge eyes

Details: - has nearly 360-degree view of world → easy to spot prey

- compound eyes can stay focused on prey

- can twist and turn in air while hunting → can keep steady eye on prey

Second Reason: mental ability

Details: - can predict route prey takes when tries to escape

- moves in that direction before prey does → is acting rather than reacting

- is faster than prey → lets it catch, kill, and eat prey

B

Sample Response Q4_09_2

The professor tells the class that the most effective predator in the world is the dragonfly. According to the professor, the dragonfly is successful ninety-five percent of the time it goes hunting. He states that there are two reasons why the dragonfly can hunt so well. One is that the dragonfly has exceptional vision thanks to its eyes. First, it can see almost everything around it. Second, even while flying, the dragonfly can keep its eyes focused on its prey. The other reason concerns the dragonfly's mental abilities. The dragonfly can predict the direction in which prey like a mosquito will fly when trying to avoid getting caught. The dragonfly then moves in that direction even before the prey does. As a result, the dragonfly can catch its prey easily.

iBT Practice Test

Listening Script

Listen to part of a lecture in a zoology class.

W Professor: Lots of animals are social, and they typically live in large groups. Naturally, not all of the animals in these groups get along with one another. In some cases, they have fights. Interestingly, scientists have observed that many animals attempt to reconcile after a fight. Let's look at a couple of animals which do that.

The spotted hyena is a highly social animal that travels in packs. Sometimes two hyenas get in a fight. In many cases, the loser attempts to reconcile with the winner within five minutes of the fight coming to an end. Attempts at reconciliation can take several forms. The loser may rub its body against the winner. The loser may also lick the other hyena. Sometimes, uh, the loser starts trying to play with the winner. These are all attempts to reconcile so that the two no longer are angry and feel like fighting.

The bottlenose dolphin is another social animal. In case you don't know, dolphins can be quite aggressive, so fights between them are not unusual. Yet dolphins often make efforts at reconciliation after fighting. This typically involves the loser swimming beside the winner and bumping into it in a friendly or affectionate manner. Sometimes the loser even tows the other dolphin through the water, uh, essentially giving it a ride through the water.

Many animals reconcile after fight

1 **spotted hyena = highly social pack animal**
   - 2 hyenas fight → loser tries to reconcile w/in 5 minutes of fight ending
   - may rub body against winner + lick other hyena
   - sometimes loser tries to play w/winner

2 **bottlenose dolphin = social animal**
   - dolphins = aggressive → fights not unusual
   - loser tries to reconcile → swims beside winner + bumps into winner
   - loser may tow winner through water → gives it ride

The professor talks about social animals which reconcile after they fight. She mentions that animals living in groups don't always get along well and occasionally fight. After fighting, some animals try to reconcile with one another. The spotted hyena does this. After a fight, the loser may do some various activities. It may rub up against the winner, lick the winner, or try to play with the winner. These are attempts to make peace between the two hyenas. The bottlenose dolphin also practices reconciliation. The loser of a fight may bump into the other dolphin in a friendly or affectionate way. The loser may also tow the other dolphin through the water. Both actions are attempts by the loser to reconcile with the winner.

Question 4 #10   p. 142

A

Listen to part of a lecture in an archaeology class.

M Professor: There are countless archaeological dig sites. Most archaeologists take great care to preserve these sites. They slowly and carefully dig and keep accurate records of everything they unearth. Yet other sites have suffered destruction. Archaeologists do this both on purpose and by accident.

Looting is probably the greatest cause of the destruction of archaeological sites. Some thieves look for ancient sites to find buried treasure. They cannot resist the lure of gold, silver, jewelry, and other artifacts. Even some professional archaeologists loot artifacts. There are collectors around the world willing to pay huge amounts of money for ancient relics. Looting in the Middle East in places such as Iran and Iraq has destroyed sites thousands of years old. It's unfortunate since some of these sites are looted by archaeologists, uh, who should preserve sites rather than destroy them.

Archaeologists can also accidentally destroy sites. Most of the time, this happens when they fail to use proper excavation methods. For example, Heinrich Schliemann, the man credited with discovering Troy, caused a great amount of damage to the dig site. Schliemann was interested in treasure. There were several layers from different time periods at the ruins of Troy. Schliemann just dug through them without making an effort to preserve them or to document his work. That caused a great amount of harm to an important dig site. Sadly, other archaeologists have harmed many sites by behaving like Schliemann.

Main Topic: the harming of archaeological sites

Main Idea: some dig sites damaged by archaeologists

First Way: looting = greatest cause of destruction

Details: - thieves want buried treasure → sometimes archaeologists loot artifacts
   - collectors pay big $ for artifacts → lots of looting in Iran and Iraq
   - destroys sites thousands of years old

Second Way: accidentally destroy sites

Details: - may fail to use proper excavation methods
   - Heinrich Schliemann discovered Troy → several layers in Troy
   - dug through ruins w/out making effort to preserve them or document work
   - caused harm to important dig site

B

The professor lectures about dig sites and how some archaeologists harm them. He comments that the destruction can be done on purpose or by accident. First, the professor discusses looting. He says some places have gold, silver, and other treasures. He remarks that some archaeologists can't resist stealing from the sites and selling treasures and artifacts to collectors. He points out that this often happens in places in the Middle East. Next, the professor states that some archaeologists aren't careful when excavating dig sites. He uses Heinrich Schliemann as an example. Schliemann excavated Troy, but he wasn't careful. There were several layers at the site, but Schliemann didn't care about them. He just dug in search of treasure. As a result, he greatly harmed the Troy site.

iBT Practice Test

Listen to part of an lecture in an archaeology class.

W Professor: In 122 A.D., the Romans began building a wall in northern England. It took six years and 15,000 men to do the work. By the time it was finished, the wall extended across the entire land from sea to sea. It was around 120 kilometers long. It would be known as Hadrian's Wall after the Roman emperor of the time, Hadrian.

The Romans wanted to separate themselves from the barbarians, uh, as they referred to the tribes living in northern England. Now, uh, what most people don't realize is that it wasn't just a simple wall. There was more to it than that. The wall itself was made of stone. It stood more than four meters high at most points. It also had towers every few hundred meters. Those helped the Romans defend themselves from invasion.

There was also a ditch dug in front of the wall. This made the height of Hadrian's Wall even more imposing. In some places, there were pits dug in the ground. Defensive measures such as sharpened sticks were placed in the ditch and the holes. This made it more difficult for attackers to reach the wall. Finally, behind the wall, there was a highway running alongside it. That enabled the Romans to send troops to trouble spots quickly whenever there was a need.

ground. The ditch and the holes often had sharp sticks in them. Last, the Romans built a highway behind the wall. The road allowed the Romans to send reinforcements to various places that needed help.

Sample Notes

Hadrian's Wall → extends across northern England

1 **Romans wanted to be separate from barbarians**
   - built wall made of stone → stood 4m high in places
   - had towers ever few 100 meters
   - let Romans defend against invasions

2 **ditch dug in front of wall**
   - made height of wall more imposing
   - holes in ground, too → sharpened sticks put in ditch and holes
   - highway by wall → let Romans send troops to trouble spots

Sample Response ⌗ Q4_10_4

The professor lectures about Hadrian's Wall. She notes that it was a wall built in northern England that went across the entire country. The Romans made it to keep the northern barbarian tribes away. First, the professor discusses the wall itself. She says that Hadrian's Wall was made of stone and was at least four meters high in many places. It also featured towers to help the Romans defend it. Next, she says there was a ditch in front of the wall. In some places, there were also holes in the

Actual Test

Question 1 p. 147

Sample Response — Agree 🎧 AT01_SR1

I think it's possible for people to have different opinions but still to be friends. In fact, one of my friends and I have opposite opinions about many things. However, we are still close. For starters, we enjoy debating each other. She tells me her thoughts and defends them. Then, I tell her what I believe and why. Because we respect each other's opinions, we get along well. It's also great to have a friend who doesn't think the same way I do. If all of my friends agreed with me, our conversations would be boring. Instead, I prefer having a friend who makes me think about my opinions and why I have them.

Sample Response — Disagree 🎧 AT01_SR2

I wish the statement were true, but I disagree with it. People with different opinions simply cannot be friends. One of my classmates and I have different opinions about lots of things. As a result, we frequently argue when we talk. There is just no way that we can be friends. Secondly, I wouldn't want to be friends with someone whose opinions are different from mine. I would think that the person is very misguided or uneducated. As a result, I could not respect him or her for having thoughts so different from mine. Instead, I think people should be friends with others who have the same opinions.

Question 2 p. 148

Listening Script

Now listen to two students discussing the letter.

M Student: Hmm . . . You know, this letter in the school newspaper makes plenty of sense.

W Student: Which one?

M: The one where the student asks for a special event so that students can sell various possessions.

W: I must have missed it. What do you think of it?

M: I think the student is onto something. I mean, uh, I've seen so many perfectly good items get thrown out, especially by graduating seniors. Last semester, somebody even threw away a racing bicycle. It should have been sold to someone who wanted it.

W: Good point.

M: Plus, many students don't have much money to buy

new things.

W: You can say that again.

M: It would really benefit them if they could buy some items, uh, such as furniture, at low prices. I mean, um, I'd love to get a sofa for my room, but I'm not going to purchase a new one. I hope the school considers this suggestion.

Sample Response 🎧 AT02_SR

The man tells the woman about a letter to the editor in the school newspaper. The writer wants the school to hold a flea market every time a semester ends. That will let students sell their unwanted items. The man speaks in favor of this idea and gives two reasons for doing so. He comments on seeing students throw away items that are still usable. He says one student even threw away a racing bicycle. He wishes people would sell the items instead. The man also remarks that students don't always have money to buy new things, so a flea market would benefit them. They would be able to acquire items such as furniture that they want, but they could pay low prices.

Question 3 p. 149

Listening Script

Now listen to a lecture on this topic in a geology class.

M Professor: Take a look at these pictures up here on the screen. Look at this . . . and this . . . These are pictures of the Badlands. It's a unique region located in the southwestern part of the state of North Dakota.

Now, uh, the Badlands is dry today, but it once had rivers and streams flowing through it. They're responsible for the erosion which created the ravines between the hills and the mounds. Now look closer. Do you see what the erosion has exposed? Notice the colorful layers in each mound. Can you see them . . . ? They are the result of stratification.

Seventy-five million years ago, the Rocky Mountains were forming. As that happened, sand, silt, and clay were spread in the Badlands. There were also nearby volcanic eruptions. They spread ash and lava on the ground. Over time, the ground was compressed, and rock layers were created. Each layer contains a different type of rock or was formed in a different way. That's why there are so many colors. Thanks to stratification, we can tell exactly how and when the rocks in the Badlands formed. It has also created one of the country's most beautiful places.

🎧 AT03_SR

In his lecture, the professor shows some pictures of mounds in the Badlands. It's a place in the state of North Dakota. The professor mentions that there are colorful layers of rocks in the mounds. He says that stratification created them. Millions of years ago, the Rocky Mountains were being created. So many different kinds of rocks as well as ash and lava from volcanoes covered the ground. They were then compressed, which made individual layers of rocks. There are many colors in the layers since different rocks were formed in various ways. According to the reading passage, stratification is when layers of rocks are formed. These layers may be very thin or thick. When the rocks are exposed, the stratification of layers is easy to see.

🎧 AT04_SR

The professor tells the class that most plants lean toward the sun because they can get more sunlight for photosynthesis. However, he mentions two reasons why some plants don't bend toward the sun. The first reason concerns water. When a plant has water on its stem and leaves, it may not bend toward the sun. By getting exposed to sunlight, the water could evaporate quickly. The plant first absorbs the water and then bends toward the sun. The second reason has to do with individual species. Vines like ivy and honeysuckle grow by attaching themselves to other plants or hard surfaces. They are therefore unable to bend toward the sun. The professor advises gardeners to make sure these vines are planted so that they'll get exposed to the sun.

Question 4

p. 150

Listening Script

Listen to part of a lecture in a botany class.

M Professor: You've all probably noticed that most plants lean toward sunlight. These plants have, uh, internal mechanisms which make that happen. In doing so, they can be exposed to the most sunlight to undergo photosynthesis. But plants don't always lean toward the sun. Let me tell you why . . .

In some instances, a plant may have moisture on its leaves and stem. This may cause it not to lean toward the sun. Plants need water to survive, so this is rather logical. After all, if a wet plant bends toward the sun, the increased heat could evaporate the moisture fairly quickly. By not bending, uh, so that it gets the maximum amount of light, the plant is protecting itself from harm. Later, after the water is absorbed or evaporates, the plant typically bends in the direction of the sun.

Some plants aren't able to lean toward the sun because they're attached to something. I'm thinking specifically of climbing plants . . . uh, you know, like ivy, honeysuckle, and wisteria. These vines usually bind themselves to other plants or to wire or wooden frames in gardens or on walls. Thus, bending toward the sun simply isn't easy for these clinging plants. Individuals who want these plants around their homes need to take care when planting them. People should plant them in places where the plants will get the most sunlight. Then, the plants won't have to lean toward the sun.